COMMITMENT CRITERIA:
23 Women Patients of Camarillo State Mental Hospital

KIRSTEN ANDERBERG

Copyright © 2011 Kirsten Anderberg

All rights reserved.

ISBN: 1466253169
ISBN-13: 978-1466253162

DEDICATION

I dedicate this book to all survivors of American institutions; but especially to the women who were placed in Camarillo Mental Hospital never to be heard from again, while their husbands' obituaries are easily found in the press. Many of the lives of women in this book were well-documented right up to their internment at Camarillo, at which point all press about them stops.

CONTENTS

	Acknowledgments	i
1	Mary B	1-3
2	Edith Boyd	4-5
3	Barbara Burns	6-10
4	Mary Kendall Curtis	11-13
5	"Connie Duke"	14-15
6	Mrs. Elizabeth Ann Duncan	16-60
7	Mrs. Gladys Baker Eley	61-62
8	43 Yr. Old Female Schizoid-Paranoid Patient	63
9	Mrs. Marjorie Haas	64
10	Deliga Harp	65
11`	Mrs. Dora Herrera	66
12	Tara Ann Katona	67-69
13	Miriam Kim	70
14	Mrs. Myrtle Nell Klinker	71
15	Joan Krieg	87
16	Ronnie Rae	88-89
17	Mrs. Frances C. Robinson	90
18	Gia Scala	91-96
19	Catherine Smith	97-98

20	Paula Stanway Thorpe	99-106
21	A Young Woman Who Took LSD and Thought She Was A Chair	107
22	Hazel Younger	108-114
23	Mrs. Virginia Evelyn Wilson	115

WARNING: GRAPHIC CONTENT

The stories in this book are graphic and often tragic. These are true stories of women who stayed in Camarillo State Mental Hospital. Some of their lives end in tragedy, some of them commit heinous crimes, some of them are just victims of cheap husbands who want to avoid alimony. The story lines in many of these women's lives do involve violence, so I just wanted to warn people, before they read these women's stories, about the intensity of the material. I have not included any gratuitous violence and have not gone into gory details regarding events of violence, as some of the Times articles I read about the events have, but the topics themselves are still raw and sobering, and I felt they warranted a warning of some kind.

1 "MARY B"

"Mary B." was a 15 year old red-haired girl who was transferred in July 1978 from the $60 a day private Deveraux School in Santa Barbara, where she had lived for 18 months and was "making progress," to Napa State Hospital at the cost of $107 a day because the state would not pay for her care at Deveraux. Mary was called "homeless" and "emotionally disturbed" by social workers and had been in a long line of institutions in her short life. From July – Sept. 1978, she cycled through a foster home, a group home, a crisis center and a private mental facility, with each rejecting her saying she was "too disturbed." In late Sept. 1978, she was put in Kern County Hospital's 24 bed psychiatric unit (which officials admit housed 36 people at times), where she stayed for 30 days and received no treatment but for medicine and did not go to school. This locked facility cost $170 a day (and the point of this article was if she had been allowed to stay for $60 a day at Deveraux, it made more sense than all that has happened and with her now being in a $170 a day facility). Kern County Hospital said she was schizophrenic and had temper tantrums. She was taken to Camarillo State Hospital's adolescent program at $130 a day but when that "failed," she was taken to Napa State Hospital. When staff from Deveraux heard she was in a state mental hospital, one said, "Oh, my god, no. She sure as hell doesn't need to be in a state hospital or a psychiatric unit. That's a shame." Another commented, "…putting her in a state institution makes no sense. She is a deprived child. She has no mother, her father is out of the picture, and she's been put in and pulled out of so many places, she is defensive." Mary was abandoned by her parents at age 11 and became a ward of Kern County Juvenile Court at that point. The situation that this girl (whose name is protected due to her age) endured, due to the government not wanting to pay Deveraux for her stay is a good example of kids who just get lost in the system.

A few days before Christmas 1978, 15 year old Mary was taken to a hearing in the court room off of the locked psychiatric ward of Kern County Hospital. She was described as "gravely disabled" by the Times, and the hearing included a parade of social workers, mental health experts, doctors, etc. discussing where this girl with no family should go. The Times reports the hearing was conducted as if the girl was not present in the room. One psychiatrist said Mary was so starved for love and attention that she ran up to everyone, including strange men, hugging and "pawing" them, and there was concern for her safety and possible exploitation due to this behavior. She was also described as "assaultive" and "aggressive" and the judge felt that she should be returned to Napa State Hospital where she had been for several weeks prior. A public defender argued she had only been sent to Napa State Hospital due to funding problems, and said she should be returned to Deveraux.

Camarillo State Hospital Bell Tower, South Quad (Photo: K. Anderberg, July 8, 2011)

In a strange twist, Mary wrote the Deveraux School a few weeks after she was removed from there, and asked them to get her a lawyer. She began working with the state public defender's office, and yet the judge in the case, Judge Nairn, said the public defender could not represent her unless the judge assigned him to her. Then the judge said Mary was "borderline mentally retarded," and "schizophrenic" and said she was not fit to choose her own attorney and insisted he would assign one to her even though it was argued she already had a client-attorney relationship with the public defender. Eventually Judge Nairn allowed the public defender to represent Mary, but the public defender filed a complaint to have the judge removed from the case due to prejudice because of things the judge had said about Mary. Judge Nairn stayed on the case, and in the end, only two witnesses were presented as the county's witnesses and both recommended Mary go to Napa State Hospital. The public defender argued to no avail that Napa State was not the best place for Mary. The Chief Psychiatrist at Napa State also said he did not think Napa was suitable for Mary. The public defender filed a petition for the case to go to jury trial in January 1979. But Mary was remanded back to Napa State Hospital's psychiatric ward for her 14th Christmas, and Judge Nairn ordered she could have no visitors but her lawyers without his permission as "visitors upset her."

LATimes, Ronald B. Taylor, Girl Caught in Mix of Prop. 13 Tangle, Nov. 6, 1978, p. B3.

LATimes, Ronald B. Taylor, Mental Patient's Battle, Dec. 17, 1978, p. 3.

2 EDITH BOYD

On June 12, 1955, the body of 68 year old Edith Boyd was found in an apparent suicide. She climbed inside an old refrigerator and slammed it shut behind her. The cause of death was suffocation. In the Times article about her death, it says she was an outpatient of Camarillo State Hospital.

LATimes, Body of Woman Found in Icebox, Jun. 14, 1955, p.2.

Isolation wards on southeast end of South Quad. Note the hills in the background are visible over the yard wall. (Photo: Kirsten Anderberg, February 19, 2011).

3 BARBARA BURNS

Barbara Burns was an actress and daughter of comedian Bob (Bazooka) Burns.

On Jan. 8, 1958, at age 19, Barbara was arrested and admitted to being addicted to drugs. She was arrested at 10 PM at her apt. on Sunset Blvd., with two other men. Burns claimed police drove her around until 4 AM questioning her, until they finally took her to a hospital for a shot as she was so sick. The press said she had once been a very beautiful young woman but now looked ill. Burns said she took 10 capsules a day, which cost her $30 a day and that she wanted to stop. She said she tried to get into a hospital for addicts but there was no room. She said she had been using "dope as her food" since April of 1957, and said the $500 a month she received from her father's estate went to one of the largest dealers in Hollywood.

When asked how she paid for a $900 a month habit with $500, she said the dealers knew she got a monthly check and relied on it, and let her slide for the rest. She thought she owed them $300 but the math looked like she owed them more like $3,000. Burns was described as emaciated and said she had been living off of burgers and sundaes. She also said she knew that being in jail was for her own good. She said her mother and brothers had disowned her and she began to panic in jail, screaming for someone to get her out of the jail and to call her attorney. When asked where she would go if let out of jail, she said she wanted to go to a "private sanitarium" to get off drugs because she said she has tried to break the habit herself and has not been able to do it. She said when she has tried to quit using drugs at her apt., she always started using again due to the anxiety, stomach cramps and cravings.

Burns said her mother would not give her money for her singing career so she went to court at age 18, and sued for money from her father's estate. She said after that she had no contact with her family and had nothing to do and nowhere to go. She said she had no friends and would to a drug store on Sunset Strip to hang out, hoping someone would talk to her. She met some people there who gave her her first shot of opiates and said from then on she was hooked. She said she was scared and alone and the drugs were the only thing she could find to stop the anxiety. She said her days began to slip by without meaning. She said she would sleep in late, watch TV, go out for a burger, and eventually she said she was up to 10 shots of heroin a day. She again pleaded for someone to get her out of the jail. She was finally released on $500 bail.

On Jan. 9, 1958, David Mack, age 26, told police he had supplied drugs to Burns but denied that he had gotten her hooked on drugs. Mack was described as an unemployed film technician and musician. Mack said he had met Burns about 5 months prior, and that he only delivered the drugs to her, never sold them to her, and he never saw the person he was delivering the drugs for. Mack called Burns a "lonely mixed-up kid." Mack said he had been addicted to heroin for 5 years, had last done heroin two days ago, said he had a two gram a day habit, and that he had been living from motel room to motel room for the last few months. He said he made $5 - $25 deliveries to Burns' apartment and that he was paid in narcotics for himself for the deliveries. He said he bought the rest of the heroin he needed monthly with money from his unemployment check.

Burns told police that Mack had delivered, not sold, about one half gram of heroin to her apt. every two weeks for several months. She said he delivered to her about 50 times and injected shots of heroin into her 10-12 times. She said that names she gave police when they questioned her were just fake names she made up as the people she named were brought into the police station for questioning. The day before Mack ended up testifying due to Burns' testimony, he had just been arraigned on charges of soliciting narcotics to a minor.

Mack was given $5000 bail and was set to appear in court the following week. Unable to make bail, Mack sat in jail until his court appearances. Burns, at her apartment out on bail, said she would not testify against Mack because she said she did not want to be the reason anyone would get sent to prison. Burns said she did not contact her mother about the recent jail time and said she had not spoken to her mother in over 2 years.

On Jan. 14, 1958, Burns failed to appear at her criminal hearing due to being in a "sanitarium." The $500 bail she had put up was forfeited and the hearing was rescheduled for the next month, on Feb. 18. Burns had been arrested on felony narcotics possession charges but due to her complaint of addiction, charges were reduced to a misdemeanor with a penalty of 3-6 months in jail.
On Jan. 16, 1958, Burns testified at Mack's trial, saying he never took money from her, only delivered, and said now that he had never given her any shots. The judge charged Mack with selling, furnishing and administering drugs to a minor, apparently due to Burns being perhaps just 18 when they began interacting. The sentence was 5 years to life in prison. His bail was lowered from $5000 to $2500 and arraignment set for Jan. 30. Burns testified he had delivered to her no more than 10 times and that the arrangements were made with someone named Nikki or Mickey.

On the stand, Burns said she would put the heroin in a spoon with water and cook it, then when it was dissolved, she would "suck it up with an eyedropper" then inject it into her veins. She said that each shot would relax her for about half an hour. Burns said she was living in a "sanitarium" and was studying drama and music. The police testified that Burns had earlier said she had gotten 50 deliveries from Mack and that he had delivered $30 batches, of $3 capsules. Police also quoted earlier questioning with Mack where he said that those amounts were true but that he had just delivered them, he had not sold them, to Burns. Police also quoted Mack as saying he collected the money then gave it over to a third party which in turn paid him in narcotics for the delivery.

On Feb. 19, 1958, Burns pleaded innocent to misdemeanor charges of narcotics addiction, and a jury trial was set for March 20. On March 31, Burns, who turned 20 years old the previous week, was arraigned on Federal charges of failing to register as a narcotics addict before leaving and entering the U.S. She was apparently arrested at San Ysidro when she was returning from a weekend in Agua Caliente with a friend, Raymond Ott, 24, who was also arrested for possession of illegal "pep" pills. Two other men were with them, were questioned and released. When Burns was asked why she did not register, she said it was because she was "asleep." She was charged with two crimes, for both leaving and returning without notifying authorities properly. Burns said a needle mark in her arm was from a blood test for marriage she had just taken and refused to identify her groom. A doctor testified she was not using narcotics. Burns was released on her own recognizance and said she had not used drugs since her release from the sanitarium in January.

On April 14, 1958, a judge found Burns was a victim of a plot to scandalize her from a local magazine. In this plot, someone planted 2 marijuana cigarettes in Burns' apt., then later, two people showed up claiming to be Federal agents and got her to talk to them. This was actually material they planned to run in their magazine. The attorney asked the courts for $3000 from Burns' estate to pay his legal fees for fixing this dilemma between Oct. 4, 1956 and Oct. 3, 1957. The attorney was able to stop the magazine from using and printing the materials illegally obtained. The courts awarded the attorney only $1250 in fees due to Burns' diminishing estate funds. There was $29, 409 in her guardianship account when it was first set up and now there was only $7,767, with a possible $2,900 still to come from an agreement when her mother relinquished parental control.

She was arrested at age 23, in June 1961, at an apartment at 7318 ½ Fountain Ave., West Hollywood. Police said they found 95 heroin capsules on the premises. Burns was arrested with Peggy Lillian Russell, aged 47, referred to as a writer, and Barbara Louise Swann, age 36, who was reportedly an artist. Burns could not make her $5,250 bail, and the other two women faced similar bail amounts.

It was noted in an L.A. Times article about this incident that Burns had been arrested several times for narcotics activity and one arrest led her to a "90 day sentence in Camarillo State Hospital." In 1961, it was revealed that Barbara was going blind.

LATimes, Cordell Hicks, "I'm Hooked," Says Daughter of Bob Burns in Dope Case, Jan. 9, 1958, p. 2.

LATimes, Barbara Burns Arrested Again, Jun. 7, 1961, p. 27.

LATimes, Barbara Burns Losing Sight, Friends Report, Jun. 19, 1961, p. 2.

LATimes, Gave Burns Girl Dope, Man Says, Jan. 10, 1958, p. 1.

LATimes, Dope Messenger Tells of Supplying Barbara Burns, Jan. 11, 1958, p. B1.

LATimes, Barbara Burns Hearing Continued to Feb. 18, Jan. 15, 1958, p. 2.

LATimes, Barbara Burns Fails to Get Suspect Free, Jan. 17, 1958, p. 2.

LATimes, Barbara Burns Enters Plea of Innocent, Feb. 20, 1958, p. C11.

LATimes, Bob Burns' Daughter Arraigned in U.S. Court, Apr. 1, 1958, p. 2.

LATimes, Barbara Burns Scandal Plot Victim, Court Says, Apr. 15, 1958, p. 2.

Southeast side of the South Quad with its unusual architecture, leading into an enclosed courtyard with only this one opening. (Photo: K. Anderberg, Feb. 19, 2011).

4 MARY KENDALL CURTIS

Mary Kendall Curtis, aged 39, was booked into the County jail in June 1953, after her 15 year old daughter, Charlotte Ury, was missing and Mrs. Curtis sent the County Probation Dept. a letter saying her daughter's body was in the desert and would never be found. Upon questioning by the police, she said it was true the girl was dead. Mrs. Curtis basically stole her daughter from a court-appointed boarding school on June 5, 1953, after she was taken from Curtis' custody for lack of parental supervision. Curtis was accused of creating an elaborate hoax which included the fake murder of her daughter, as she was angry her daughter had been taken from her by the courts. She told the police her daughter's body had been wrapped in a yellow blanket once it got cold, and left in the desert. Curtis said that her daughter went to sleep peacefully, and that God and Jesus would forgive her.

The police noticed that Curtis' 1957 green Ford coupe with a skull and bones symbol on the trunk was missing and yet she had no explanation for its whereabouts. Curtis was arrested at the headquarters for a "cult" named the "Contenders for the Crown," which was said to be a group which helped destitute mothers and she was said to be a missionary for the group. She supposedly founded the group which had 30 current members. According to the authorities who ran the court-appointed boarding school her daughter attended, Curtis had never taken her daughter from the school before the current visit which ended in the girl going missing. Curtis had told the school she wanted to take her daughter out to buy her ballerina slippers, but the court order said the girl had to spend nights at the school. Curtis had another daughter, who was 13 years old, and custody of that daughter was given to Curtis' mother, and Curtis lived with her mother, and thus also the 13 year old girl, whose custody had been removed from her. Police reports showed that Curtis had been in the General Hospital psychiatric ward for observations for a week recently then was released.

On June 11, 1953, police pressed charges against Curtis for suspicion of murder of her daughter after she sent the County Probation Dept. a bizarre letter saying her daughter was dead and they would never find her. The letter was basically in revenge for the state taking her daughter from her custody and said things such as if Curtis could not have her then nobody could and said the girl was dead and left in the desert. The letter was dated June 8, but the Probation Dept. received it on June 11, at which time they arrested Curtis. On June 12, 1953, Curtis was jailed and admitted to the District Attorney that she made up the hoax of her daughter's murder as revenge on the Juvenile Courts for taking the custody of her children away. There was some speculation the girl had gone to Catalina Island via Long Beach and police there said they checked hotels, rooming houses and beaches on the island. Curtis said since she could not get a court hearing, the only thing left "was war to the finish." She refused to say where her 15 year old daughter was. Another place they looked for the girl was at the cult headquarters.

On June 13, Curtis was forced into court with the same judge that ruled her children had to be removed from her custody and demanded she tell where the child was and if she was alive or dead. Curtis refused to answer saying "I don't want you to have her, I don't want anyone to have her, it is too late now." The judge ordered her to 5 days in County jail for contempt of court to which she retorted with hysterical laughter. Curtis purportedly offered to tell where the girl was in exchange for an apology for the state removing her children from her custody. She stated her daughter was alive. Curtis' mother was brought to the stand and testified her daughter had discussed a plot to kidnap her daughter back from the school but did not believe she would kill the girl. The mother insisted Curtis was just being dramatic in trying to force her point. Curtis angered prosecutors when she proposed her apology for daughter deal and the judge sent her back to jail for contempt for her actions. Curtis said her husband had abandoned her and her two children when the children were young, then he returned in 1946 and supposedly died the night he returned to her. She said she then turned to spiritualism. A man who was in the cult with Curtis and had gone with her to Las Vegas the previous week testified he had not seen the missing girl. Curtis is described by the LA Times in 1953, as a "39 year old self-styled mystic."

On June 13, 1953, the daughter was found on a ranch in the Anza area, around Hemet, after a 3 day state wide search. She had been there since June 5, when she left the school with her mother. She was found by police investigators. When found, the missing 15 year old told police she had been "riding horses, playing with a dog and having fun." The owners of the ranch, Mr. and Mrs. Schmoll, had no idea the girl had been kidnapped and just thought it was a visit. Mr. Schmoll was a forest ranger who met Mrs. Curtis through her sister, Mrs. Irene McCaulous. The Schmolls said Mrs. Curtis had left the girl with them, promising to pay $10 a week for her keep there. The ranger's radio was reportedly out of batteries, thus he did not have access to the news.

On June 15, 1953, the District Attorney filed charges against Mary Curtis for contributing to the delinquency of a minor, and she remained in jail for contempt of court since June 12, when she was sentenced to 5 days in jail. The D.A. said he would be requesting a mental evaluation of Curtis at this time.

On July 3, 1953, Curtis was committed to Camarillo State Hospital after a psychopathic hearing at the General Hospital. Superior Judge William P. Haughton signed the commitment papers. Curtis' daughter was returned to the juvenile home 10 days after she went missing. Mary was charged with contributing to the delinquency of a minor but the hearing was postponed due to her confinement in Camarillo Hospital.

LATimes, Mother Jailed as Girl Disappears in Mystery, Jun. 12, 1953, p. 1.

LATimes, Skull and Crossbones Painted on Car, Jun. 13, 1953, p. 1.

LATimes, Girl in Hoax Found Hiding Near Anza, Jun. 14, 1953, p. 1.

LATimes, Charge Filed in Girl Slaying Hoax, Jun. 16, 1953, p. 12.

LATimes, Mother in Murder Hoax Committed to Hospital, Jul. 4, 1953, p. 3.

5 "CONNIE DUKE"

On Christmas Day 1975, a 14 year old girl kidnapped a 6 month old baby from an apartment she was visiting on Christmas. Karla Simmons, the 21 year old mother of the baby, said she and her son were visiting a family in Anaheim and they left the baby with "Connie" when they went to the store. "Connie" said she got to the apartment because she was hitchhiking on Christmas and the people who picked her up took her to the apartment, not knowing her. When they returned from the store, 15 minutes later, the baby, diapers, and the 14 year old girl were gone. The girl said she liked the baby and wanted it. She hitchhiked with the baby from Anaheim, asking to be taken to Knott's Berry Farm, but the park was closed. She then asked the person who picked her up hitchhiking with the baby to take her somewhere she could get emergency assistance. The driver, Gregory Lubben, 24, then took her to Norwalk Community Hospital. The hospital said they could not help her, so she asked to be driven to an apt. in Santa Ana where she said her brother lived.

When police arrived, she tried to hide the child between the refrigerator and some cupboards. Police retrieved the baby unharmed. She told police her name was Connie Duke and that she was 19 years old. In time, she admitted she was 14 years old and that Connie Duke was not her real name. (Due to her age, her real name was not published.) She was taken to the Orange County Juvenile Hall awaiting a hearing. This girl lived at Camarillo State Mental Hospital for three years prior to the babynapping, and did not return to Camarillo after her Thanksgiving "furlough."

LATimes, Baby Recovered Unhurt, Texas Woman Arrested, Dec. 29, 1975, p. 3.

LATimes, Steve Emmons, Suspect, 14, is Mental Patient, Dec. 31, 1975, p. C3.

Murals line the hall in the adolescent/children's buildings in the North Quad. Pictured are characters from the TV show Fantasy Island, Michael Jackson, Marilyn Monroe, the Marx Brothers, Diana Ross and others. (Photo: K. Anderberg, Dec. 29, 2011)

6 MRS. ELIZABETH ANN DUNCAN

In Dec. 1958, at age 54, Mrs. Elizabeth Ann Duncan was accused of hiring two men to kill the "pretty wife" of her attorney son, Frank P. Duncan. Her daughter-in-law, a nurse named Olga Kupezyk Duncan, aged 30, was missing as of Nov. 17, 1958, and it was reported that Olga was constantly threatened by Elizabeth, according to Olga's father. Olga's father said Olga had written them about violence and threats from Elizabeth ever since she got married to Elizabeth's son. Olga came to the U.S. in Nov. 1957, and met the Duncans in December 1957. Olga married Elizabeth's son, Frank, in July 1958 and within 2 weeks, they were separated. Olga said Elizabeth would come to her apt. while her husband was at work and threaten her and it got so bad, that she was too afraid and separated from Frank. The last letter her parents received from Olga was dated Nov. 12, 1958. On Nov. 27, 1958, two weeks before the investigation about his wife's murder began, Frank Duncan quit his job at a Santa Barbara law firm, moved out of the apartment he shared with his mother, Elizabeth, and began living in an apartment in Hollywood under a fake name.

Frank and Olga Duncan were married in June, 1958. Olga was the nurse attending Frank's mother, Elizabeth, at Cottage Hospital in Santa Barbara, and the two became romantically involved after that meeting. At that time, Elizabeth had been hospitalized due to her taking an overdose of sleeping pills in a suicide attempt and being in a coma for 4 days at Cottage Hospital.

COMMITMENT CRITERIA

On August 8, 1958, Elizabeth went to an attorney's office, saying she was Olga and a man named Ralph that she brought with her posed as her son Frank and she asked the attorney to draw up annulment papers for the marriage, saying it had not been consummated. Later, the man who was thought to be "Ralph" was identified by Elizabeth's 84 year old neighbor, Mrs. Short. Mrs. Short said that she had met the man named Ralph with Elizabeth and that he complained all the time about having to pay child support. Police collected photos of men who were behind on their child support, showed them to Short, and she identified the man known as Ralph, whose real name is Frank Winterstein, age 25, of Santa Maria. A warrant was issued for his arrest on Dec. 18, 1958, for crimes of perjury and forgery. Fearing for her safety, Mrs. Short was taken by police to an undisclosed location to go into hiding. It was later revealed that Mrs. Short had told police about the plot to kill Olga on Dec. 12, and thus she was a star witness and it was important that she was placed in hiding.

On Aug. 9, a judge approved the annulment unaware of the falsification. A few days later, Elizabeth's son, Frank, an attorney, learned of the annulment. Olga was no longer living with Frank at this time. Elizabeth was questioned by police then held as a suspect involved with her daughter-in-law's disappearance. Elizabeth was charged with four felonies for these false annulment attempts in Ventura County. Olga had been missing for a month at this point and was pregnant. Police then arrested Augustine Baldonado, 25, and Lewis E. Moya, 22, as both were also suspected as having something to do with Olga's disappearance. Frank, Elizabeth's son, showed up for her hearing and asked the courts to reduce her $50,000 bail to no avail.

On Dec. 18, 1958, Elizabeth's bail was reduced from $50,000 to $5,000 after her son argued on her behalf, saying there was no evidence to tie her to Olga's disappearance and if the courts felt there was, he demanded proof be immediately presented. Frank was often seen walking hand and hand into the courtrooms with his mother and Elizabeth refused to comment on anything in the courtroom on the advice of her son. Frank commented at this point that he believed his wife was still alive. He also commented that at some time Olga had threatened to bring him unpleasant publicity but said he felt this would "be going to the extreme." He said he never went to Olga's apt. to clean it up after she went missing, and said he had never heard of his mother making threats to Olga. Frank said he planned on living with his wife in the future and commented that his mother "hindered" his marriage's "development." Frank said his mother showed surprise when he told her she was missing, and he said he cross-examined his own mother and was convinced she knows nothing about Olga's disappearance.

Elizabeth had a strange past with annulments and marriages of her own. She married her first husband, Frank, in San Diego, on April 24, 1932. A San Mateo attorney also informed the court in 1958 at the odd annulment trial, that Elizabeth had married a man named Joseph Gold in San Francisco, using her maiden name, Elizabeth Lowe. They separated a few hours later, and were divorced on Oct. 6, 1950. There were also reports that Elizabeth had married Benjamin Young Vincent Cogbill in San Francisco in July, 1953 and their marriage was annulled on Oct 3, 1953. The San Mateo attorney also testified that he had received a petition for an annulment from a George Satriano, against Elizabeth, in 1953. Elizabeth and George had been married in San Francisco on Dec. 15, 1951, and they separated within a few months. During those hearings, the San Mateo attorney testified that Frank was a student at Hastings Law School and he sat in the front row. The judge refused to give the marriage an annulment, but a divorce was granted to Elizabeth and George on July 23, 1953.

In 1954, Elizabeth married a 27 year old Marine, who was described as "good looking" and was her son's classmate. Stephen S. Gillis later sued Elizabeth for an annulment due to a loveless marriage that had not been consummated. Gillis claimed Elizabeth said they could not consummate the marriage until after her son graduated from law school because "it might disturb him." Elizabeth somehow argued she had given Gillis a baby daughter in Santa Barbara but the judge did not believe her and granted Gillis the annulment after purportedly lecturing Gillis about making bad choices in life.

Elizabeth was also sued for an annulment by Leonard Joseph Sollenne, a Santa Barbara contractor, on Oct. 2, 1957. Leonard said that she said she would inherit a large amount of money from an ex-husband if she remarried and made a deal to split the money with Leonard. He said they got married on Aug. 12, 1957 in San Francisco and separated on Sept. 1, 1957, when he realized she was not inheriting money as she said. Frank once again represented his mother and on Oct. 3, he said Elizabeth had agreed to the annulment but then the following day, Elizabeth changed her mind and hired a different attorney and filed a demurrer to the annulment (she tried to have the annulment dropped). Leonard changed his claim for annulment from her fraud of finances then to her defrauding him of her age, saying she was 44 and of child bearing age, when in reality she was 54, and unable to bear children. At the trial on Oct. 9, 1958, Elizabeth did not show up for the hearing and Leonard was given the annulment by the judge.

By Dec. 19, 1958, blood had been found in a sedan that was suspected as an accessory to the disappearance of Olga. The car was registered to a Santa Barbara woman, Mrs. Esperanza Esquivel, and was found 3 blocks from Olga's apartment. Part of the back seat cover was also missing. A soiled gray overcoat was also found in the car and was tested by L.A. Police Dept. chemists. Esquivel said the blood in the car was from a butchered pig her husband had carried in the car from a ranch. Frank, Elizabeth's son, had previously defended Esquivel's husband in a receiving stolen property case. Esquivel said Elizabeth had been in the Paradise Café, which she owned, a week prior to Olga's disappearance. Later, police reports would show Mrs. Esquivel was reluctant to cooperate with police and was known to have narcotics sales and receiving of stolen property at her café and police were actively trying to shut down her café while also using her as a witness against players in the murder plot. Mrs. Esquivel was later said to have been the person who introduced Elizabeth to her two accomplices.

On Dec. 19, 1958, Elizabeth was accused by police of hiring Augustine Baldonado, 25, and Lewis E. Moya, 22, for $3,000 each, to kill Olga. Baldonado later said Elizabeth only paid them a couple hundred dollars in the end. Due to information police obtained from the accomplices, they knew that Olga's body had been disposed of at a construction site on Nov. 18, between midnight and 5 AM. The police made a plea to the public for help in locating the gravesite. Elizabeth remained in Ventura County Jail for the annulment fraud charges as the murder investigation continued and Baldonado was in the same jail held for nonpayment of child support. Both of them were waiting for sentencing on their previous crimes and had a $100,000 bail each put on them and would be moved later to Santa Barbara for the new charges of conspiracy to murder up there. Moya was also in jail at this time on a parole violation. By this time, the FBI were also involved. Elizabeth's son was seen in the media saying his mother would be out of jail at any moment and he also went to the Santa Barbara Police Station, requesting a meeting with the police chiefs there, but neither were available so he left. While authorities looked throughout Santa Barbara and Ventura Counties for any sign of Olga, a city clerk in Monterey who was unable to collect a debt from Elizabeth began an extensive study into her past. This investigation into her past, as collected by the Monterey city clerk, was given to a Santa Barbara attorney named Stanley Tomlinson. The file on Elizabeth given to Tomlinson included 7 aliases Elizabeth was known to use.

On Dec. 22, 1958, Olga's body was found in a shallow grave near Casitas Pass. Baldonado had confessed to police and led them to the grave. Since Olga was almost 9 months pregnant, Elizabeth, Moya and Baldonado were all charged with two murders each. Baldonado finally confessed that he and Moya had kidnapped Olga at gunpoint from her apartment sometime after midnight and police said she fought with her captors once in the car. Moya later said that he had tricked Olga into coming down to the car to help them bring her husband upstairs and when she went down to help, they hit her over the head with the gun. Baldonado said he drove the car with Olga and Moya down Highway 101 to Carpinteria then took Highway 150 up to the Lake Casitas Dam project. Ten miles north of Oak View, Baldonado got out of the car and dug a shallow grave down a ravine as Moya guarded the woman in the car. When Baldonado returned to the car, Olga was fighting with Moya. Baldonado beat Olga unconscious with the gun, saying he was going to shoot her but the beating of her with the gun had damaged it and it would no longer shoot. He then said Moya strangled Olga to death. Police said Olga's body did bear the signs of the beatings and strangulations, that it was not clear if she was dead when she was buried, and that she was dressed in a bathrobe. The grave site was a few yards from a spot where Summerland resident Cecil Lambert told police he had seen someone digging a grave a few days earlier. As these murder charges were filed, Frank hired attorney S. Ward Sullivan, who was a well-known defense attorney, to defend his mother. Frank and Sullivan met with Elizabeth for two hours in jail, then Frank constructively went into hiding, leaving the Santa Barbara area with no forwarding address at his law office or home. Two of the witnesses in the trial, Mrs. Esquivel, and Mrs. Short, were now in hiding also. Olga's father, a Canadian National Railroad foreman from Manitoba, Canada, ended up finding out about his daughter's death from the Associated Press, not the police.

On Dec. 23, 1958, Frank Duncan was subpoenaed as a witness to the grand jury investigation of Olga's murder. Los Angeles Police began a search for Frank when he could not be located. The attorney Frank hired to represent his mother also said he did not know where Frank was and had last spoken to him on Dec. 20. Frank was also being sought by attorneys trying to sort out Olga's financial affairs after her death as she was still legally married to Frank. Apparently Frank had shared an apt. with his mother after Olga left him and his name was still on the lease of the apt. he and Olga had moved into, but the landlord said he stayed somewhere else and only came to pick up clothes. She had last seen him on Dec. 21. On Dec. 24, 1958, Elizabeth was pictured in the LATimes smiling in her horned-rim glasses looking more like a lunch lady than a murderer, as she answered questions for the media about the murder of Olga which she denied any part of.

Four to five other people were offered money by Elizabeth to kill Olga and all of them gave statements against Elizabeth for the grand jury trial which began on Dec. 26, 1958. Elizabeth tried to claim she was being blackmailed by Moya and Baldonado and had no part in the murder plot. Moya also claimed innocence and said nothing. An ex-client of Frank's claimed to see Frank speeding south of the Mexico border on Dec. 23, 1958. Reports said Olga's body would be released to her father who was flying in from Canada if her husband, Frank, was not located by the time the father showed up.

On Dec. 25, 1958, Christmas, Frank was finally located in a Hollywood apartment and served the subpoena for the Ventura County grand jury trial on Dec. 26. On Christmas at midnight, Moya confessed to the murder, the night before the grand jury trial. Fifteen witnesses were presented to the jury, including Frank, and the jury took only 15 minutes to indict Baldonado, Moya and Elizabeth on conspiracy, kidnapping and murder charges. Elizabeth was also charged with 4 felony crimes for the annulment fraud, along with Ralph Winterstein, her accomplice, whom she paid $60 for his services. A warrant was issued for Ralph after the grand jury trial and his bail was set at $50,000. As the grand jury trial went on, Frank was seen shaking and nervous waiting with other witnesses and the press. Frank was called into the grand jury to testify for an hour and 40 minutes mostly about his mother's history and her past annulments. Pacing the hallways, Frank was asked by reporters if he thought his mom was guilty of Olga's murder and he said he just did not know but that he knew of no past history of his mother's where she would be able to kill things, he said she was never cruel. The Grand Jury indictments set no bail for Elizabeth, Moya and Baldonado, and set a bail amount for Elizabeth's annulment fraud charges at $50,000. Arraignment hearings for the murder charges were set for Dec. 30.

Part of the Grand Jury case against Elizabeth was the testimony of Rudolph Romero, age 27, a "kitchen worker." He said Elizabeth offered him $2500 to kill Olga in her own apt., put her body in the bathtub and pour lye over it to dispose of it. Romero declined the offer.

On Dec. 29, Olga's father met Frank, his son-in-law for the first time, and reportedly Frank sobbed like a baby and Olga's father was also speechless in tears. Both met to arrange Olga's funeral as Elizabeth sat in jail for Olga's murder. Frank continued to pay S. Ward Sullivan to represent his mother in the trial. Olga's mother was hospitalized due to her extreme grief due to her daughter's death and did not come to the U.S. with her husband. Olga also had one sister and her brother came to CA with her father to help prepare funeral arrangements. Even up to this late date, Elizabeth denied all knowledge of the murder, and claimed Moya and Baldonado were blackmailing her, extorting money from her (the fees she paid them), and were now trying to frame her for a murder.

On Dec. 31, 1958, Elizabeth was arraigned on murder charges. More facts about the Grand Jury investigation and hearing were revealed. In the Grand Jury indictment, it came out that Frank knew of a plot in which his mother was trying to kill his wife back in August of 1958, 2 months after they were married. Mrs. Barbara Reed, a Santa Barbara carhop, testified that Elizabeth offered her $1500 to pour acid on Olga and push her off a cliff. Reed testified that she had known Elizabeth for 10 years, and that she had asked Reed to "get rid of" Olga because she was "interfering with Frank's future." Reed said Elizabeth asked her to ring Olga's doorbell, then to throw acid in her face, and then Elizabeth would throw a blanket over Olga, kidnap her and throw her over a cliff somewhere. She told Elizabeth she would consider the offer, and then immediately contacted Frank Duncan, Elizabeth's son and Olga's husband, about the murder plot his mother had revealed to her. Mrs. Reed said she insisted that Frank do something, saying his mother had gone mad and that Olga was in danger. Frank reportedly responded, "you know it, too." Reed said she told Frank he needed to remove Olga from the situation for she was in danger and that Frank acted like it was nobody else's business and that he would take care of it. Frank's countertestimony to this was to say that Reed had only told him of a plot to kidnap Olga by his mother, and that when he asked his mother if such a thing happened, she denied it. Frank said he just thought the plot was so ridiculous that it was fictional and told his mother to behave lest she get them into embarrassing situations. Frank further elaborated that he took no precautions to move Olga to a place of safety as he "couldn't believe" it was required. Frank also said that his mother disapproved of his marriage to Olga.

At the Dec. 31 arraignment, Elizabeth's attorney asked for a day's extension on the case before entering her plea, and the judge granted an extension until the following day. The arraignment for the two codefendants that she hired was also moved to the next day, as it was said the men were poor and without means to hire legal representation as Elizabeth had. The judge assigned attorneys to the two men, and the District Attorney in the case, Mr. Gustafson, said he was not willing to consider anything but the death penalty for all three on trial. Gustafson said it would take about 6 weeks to prepare for trial. While the arraignment was going on, Olga's 15 minute funeral was attended by her father, brother, husband Frank, and two friends from Los Angeles. She was then cremated at Ivy Lawn Memorial Park.

It was noted that Elizabeth's demeanor at this arraignment hearing was "calm and cheerful" but that she was annoyed when sent back to the jail with her codefendants. She was said to stand back, trying not to be photographed walking with Moya and Baldonado when leaving the courtroom and even grasped a windowsill trying to resist going back to jail with the deputy on duty. She then threw her hands over her face and ran towards the jail, keeping her hands over her face while Baldonado and Moya smoked a cigarette, waiting with her for the elevator to take them back to jail. It was reported that Frank had not visited his mother in jail since Olga's body had been found but Elizabeth's attorney said he intended to visit his mother soon.

The 249 page Grand Jury transcript also revealed that Elizabeth had bought a gun in September 1958 and had threatened to kill herself with it. Frank testified he took the gun from his mother, but then returned it to her when she promised to return it to the pawn shop where she bought it. Apparently the Grand Jury spent considerable time probing the relationship between

Frank and his mother. Frank said there was nothing "unnatural" about their relationship but a close family friend, and witness to the case, Mrs. Short, claimed otherwise. Frank said his mother told him, on Nov. 22, that two men were blackmailing her. D.A. Gustafson said that Elizabeth pawned jewelry on Nov. 13, and gave the $175 she obtained to Moya and Baldonado as a down payment on the murder. Elizabeth had said she did not tell her son about the blackmailing as she did not want to upset him as he was grieving over Olga's death, but Olga's body was not yet found so he would not have been grieving and thus began the unraveling of Elizabeth's story. Frank continued to be in denial that his mother could do such a thing all the way through the Grand Jury hearing and said if his mother did do such a thing, it was due to insanity.

The Grand Jury transcripts, released on Dec. 31, contained questions and answers from the D.A. to Moya and some of this dialogue was published in the LATimes. The Times reports the transcripts have Moya saying he suggested kidnapping Olga on the street and driving her in a car to Tijuana to "get rid of her." Moya said then Elizabeth said she had acid and rope, and suggested the acid be used to disfigure Olga's features, mouth and fingerprints. Moya said Elizabeth had said she hated her daughter-in-law for "blackmailing" her son. Moya said they rented a car for $25 from Baldonado's girlfriend, who later became a witness in the case, and they borrowed a gun from a friend. Moya said they drove to Olga's apt., and Baldonado stayed in the car. Moya went up to Olga and told her her husband was drunk in the back of the car, with a lot of money on him and he had asked to be taken to that address and they needed her help to get him upstairs and out of their car. When she arrived at the car, Baldonado hit her over the head with a .22 pistol, she screamed and they both threw her into the car. Moya said he drove down Highway 101 towards Highway 33 with Olga screaming the whole way. He said Baldonado was trying to hit her over the head to make her stop screaming but could not knock her out. Finally, Moya pulled the car over, and after a few heavy blows from Moya, she passed out, at which time, Moya drove and Baldonado began to wrap Olga's hands and mouth in tape. Moya said he looked for places to place the body around Ojai, and that finally he stopped somewhere, and they dragged Olga out of the car, still alive. He said they dragged her down a ravine and hit her over the head again with the gun, trying to get her to pass out, and that they had damaged the gun by hitting her with it and it would no longer shoot.

Moya said he then began digging "a hole," not a grave, as they did not have a shovel. As they dug the hole, Olga was still struggling. They agreed to strangle her since they could no longer shoot her with the gun. They said they strangled her, assumed she was dead, and buried her. They then returned to Santa Barbara, changed their clothes, ripped out the bloody back seat, and paid the woman they rented the car from for damages. When the two then asked for pay from Elizabeth, she said she could not pay them as things had not gone as she had planned. Moya then testified that he did not know Olga was pregnant and if he had known that, he does not believe he would have committed the murder.

Baldonado's Grand Jury testimony differed slightly from Moya's, saying he never hit Olga with a gun and that there were no plans of where to dispose of the body and that he kept putting the kidnapping off, wanting to avoid it. Baldonado claimed Moya strangled Olga, while Moya claimed that Baldonado strangled her.

Also in these newly released Grand Jury transcripts was testimony from Mrs. Dowhower, who said that Elizabeth asked her to date her son, Frank, and tried to get Dowhower to go with her to Lover's Lane spots in town to try to find her son and his wife. Dowhower testified that she had just recently met Elizabeth at a doctor's office and that Elizabeth would show her pictures of Frank and keep trying to get her to go to dinner with Frank, to become his girlfriend or wife as Elizabeth knew he was seeing someone, and she did not know who, but wanted it to stop. Dowhower said Elizabeth got too pushy about it, so she never did have the date with Frank.

Frank and Olga's landlady at the Garden Street apt. where Olga was eventually kidnapped from, Mrs. Dorothy Barnett, also testified against Elizabeth. She said that Olga was tormented and harassed by her mother-in-law. She said the couple rented the apt. on August 14, and a few days later, Elizabeth showed up, demanded to be given access to the apt. and said the couple was living in sin. The landlady did not accommodate Elizabeth and told her to let them live their own lives. Elizabeth then told her she would never leave them alone, that Olga would not "have him," and that she would kill Olga if it was the last thing she did. Dorothy testified she had no idea that Elizabeth actually meant what she had said.

Mrs. Short, a 20 year friend of Elizabeth's, also testified before the Grand Jury. She said that Elizabeth had told her that Frank would not marry Olga, but once he did marry her, Elizabeth then told Mrs. Short that Frank would never live with Olga, that she would kill her first. Mrs. Short then said that Elizabeth contacted an attorney, Mr. Lynch, and told him that Olga was taking money that Elizabeth should have for her own keep and that Olga was a bad influence on Frank, was a foreigner, and needed to be "taken care of, destroyed." Mrs. Short said she was there when Elizabeth had this conversation with Mr. Lynch. Short said the attorney Lynch then told Elizabeth she would get the electric chair for such a thing, and Short said they then left, and Elizabeth was still undaunted, that she wanted to kill Olga. Short testified that Elizabeth vocalized several plots to Short, all of which Short, of course, rejected. Short said once Elizabeth suggested Short get Olga to her house, then get her to sit with her back to the closet, then Elizabeth would come out from the closet behind her with a rope and strangle her to death, while also throwing poison in her eyes. When asked if Short ever mentioned any of this to Frank, she said no. She said she found Frank to be unapproachable, and had little conversation with him ever. The judge asked Short if Frank was close to his mother and if they had shown "displays of affection," and Short said yes. The transcripts then supposedly went into detail about the mother-son relationship according to Short, but details were left out of Times reporting up to this date.

Mrs. Diane Romero also testified in the Grand Jury transcripts. Her husband was being defended by Frank, as his attorney, on narcotics possession charges. Diane said that Elizabeth had begun saying she did not like Olga and wanted to get rid of her. Diane said before Elizabeth began talking about trying to kill Olga, she gave Diane $5 to buy lye for her at a store. Later, Elizabeth would say to Diane that she wanted to use the lye to put in a bathtub with Olga's body to dissolve it so she would not be recognizable. Later, Diane testified that Elizabeth offered her husband, Rudi, money to kill Olga. Rudi also testified this was true.

Frank's part of the Grand Jury transcript took up 56 pages. Half of those pages were about his background, education, and career as well as his knowledge of his mother's numerous marriages and annulments. Frank said he began dating Olga in January and that he told his mother and she seemed fine with it. He said his mother did not want him to get married, though, not personally about Olga, but in general, she just did not want him to get married. Frank then said after he married Olga, he lived part time with Olga and part time with his mother. In August when the couple got the Garden Street apt. together, Frank said he went home each night to his wife, with a few exceptions. The judge asked why Frank did not just live with his wife, as would be expected. Oddly, Frank did not answer the question but instead said his mother would call Olga at work, and him at his office, but that he had agreed "to stay home (with Olga) until shortly before the baby arrived." The judge then interrupted and asked Frank when he first knew Olga was pregnant and Frank declined to answer saying her death was painful and he would rather not speak of it as he found it irrelevant, though he did assert to the judge that the baby was his.

The judge asked Frank if his mother owned a gun and Frank said she had bought one after he married Olga and that she had threatened to kill herself with it, which alarmed Frank. He said he took the gun from her, but then gave it back to her as she said she would return it to the pawn shop where she bought it. Frank said she had said she wanted to kill herself because she was so unhappy and because he had "changed." When asked if his mother ever told him she wanted to kill Olga, he replied that she had not. The judge asked Frank when he first heard of his mother's story of extortion by Moya. He said she told him the Saturday after the Tuesday Olga went missing that two Mexican men, whose names she did not know, were trying to blackmail her. He said he wanted to go right down to Mrs. Esquivel's café to speak to the men, but his mom said he should call the police, so he did so, that night.

On Jan. 3, 1959, the Times reported Elizabeth's attorney, Mr. Sullivan was requesting a change of venue, saying that the statements the D.A. had made to the press had swayed public opinion. He said she could no longer get a fair trial in Ventura due to this. At this point, Elizabeth had still not entered a plea of guilty or innocent. The two codefendents' court appointed attorneys also asked for a change of venue based on inflammatory statements by D.A. Gustafson.

On Jan. 6, 1959, Elizabeth's attorney, Mr. Sullivan, entered a plea of not guilty by reason of insanity on her behalf to the courts. The court was filled with 300 spectators, with standing room only, and there were gasps when the plea was entered. The judge set the murder trial date to begin on Feb. 16, but appointed Dr. Louis Nash and Dr. Phillip May of Camarillo State Mental Hospital to examine her and prepare a report on her "sanity" for the courts. Sullivan also entered a plea of not guilty by reason of insanity for each of the four lingering felony charges due to her pretending to be Olga in the false annulment hearing. The judge set the false annulment case to go to court on March 23. Sullivan's attempt at a change of venue failed as he had not served the D.A. with paperwork on the matter in the necessary fashion.

On Jan. 8, 1959, the Times reported the "first sanity tests," the "first of several examinations," had taken place. Elizabeth spoke to Dr. May, but then refused to speak with him further until talking to her attorney. Dr. Louis Nash, the other court appointed doctor to examine Elizabeth was scheduled to see her the following week. Since Elizabeth was refusing to speak to Dr. May, he suggested another doctor from Agnew State Hospital be brought in, but her attorney Sullivan said he would only allow Elizabeth to be examined by the doctors the court had appointed. Sullivan said he would straighten things out by telling Elizabeth to submit to the mental examination.

On Jan. 18, 1959, the man Elizabeth had used to pose as Frank in the fake annulment hearing, Ralph Winterstein, was located and arrested by the FBI in New Orleans. He had been indicted to appear at the Dec. 26 Grand Jury hearing, but instead left the state. Apparently Elizabeth met Winterstein by calling the Salvation Army for someone to come to her home to do an "odd job." The odd job was to pose as her son in the annulment hearing and the 26 year old "transient" did the "job." He had left town before Olga's body had been found.

On Feb. 10, 1959, both codefendents also plead not guilty due to insanity following the lead set by Elizabeth. Baldonado, age 25, had his sanity hearing set for April 6. Moya, age 20, had his sanity trial set for April 20. This legal move also set their hearings apart from Elizabeth's trial for the murder, leaving her on trial alone for the first time, without these two codefendents. The insanity pleas of these two also complicated their use as witnesses against Elizabeth.

On Feb. 16, 1959, Elizabeth entered the courtroom defiant in her horn-rimmed glasses and bouffant hairdo, "smiling and confident," according to reporters. She reportedly was greeted by her doting son, she fixed his tie, then posed for pictures with him. Frank was still in denial, insisting his mother did not commit the crime. Frank sat in the first row behind the attorneys during the trial and was subpoenaed by the prosecution as a witness and said he would probably testify for the defense as well. As jury selection advanced, another scandal erupted as a prisoner in jail with Elizabeth reported she was saving up her sleeping pills in jail to kill herself if she is found guilty. Elizabeth said she is taking doctor prescribed sleeping pills in jail but the claims of her intent to commit suicide were "unfounded." She said she was not allowed to even talk to other prisoners, but after this, all of the prisoners that Elizabeth had served time with were rumored to have been subpoenaed by the D.A. The D.A. would not confirm or deny but said he had indeed subpoenaed 100 witnesses but was not sure how many he would bring to the trial. Julia Price was in jail in Ventura County for forgery and was served with the subpoena for the trial while serving time in Corona Women's Prison. The D.A. also said at least one of the men hired to kill Olga would testify as witnesses at the trial.

The trial began on Feb. 16 with jury selection. 150 prospective jurors were told the trial would last approximately 4 weeks. Nine of the first perspective 16 jurors were dismissed because they said they had opinions which made them unable to give Elizabeth a fair trial. Sullivan again raised the issue of changing venue but the judge said they would try to find a jury and if they could not, then he would consider a change of venue. The prospective jurors took up the entire courtroom, but as jurors were dismissed, spectators took their seats. Twice during these proceedings the judge had to admonish the audience to be silent as they were giggling in response to potential jurors' answers to the attorneys' questions.

On Feb. 18, there were some arguments about the dismissal of potential jurors who do not approve of the death sentence, but the seating of jurors who admitted prejudice towards Elizabeth's guilt. The judge allowed three jurors to be seated even though they said they believed Elizabeth was guilty. But when two of these same jurors later said they also objected to the death sentence, the judge dismissed them. Three other potential jurors were dismissed for objecting to the death penalty as well. The D.A. accepted 7 jurors but the defense rose objections to each of them. By the end of the day, the defense had used up 11 of the 20 challenges allowed to keep jurors off a pool, while the D.A. had used only one of his 20 allowed challenges. The D.A. got all but one of the jurors he had approved who said they believed

Elizabeth guilty to say they would judge in the end on the facts and evidence in the case, not on their opinions. The one who would not agree to that was still kept in the jury pool, over Sullivan's objections. At one point during the jury selection proceedings, the D.A. pulled out a picture of Moya and Baldonado and Elizabeth seething with anger, calling them "liars."

On Feb. 19, the fourth day of trial, attorney A.L. Wirin, from the American Civil Liberties Union (ACLU), petitioned the court to appear as a "friend of the court" to argue for a change of venue. The judge granted the attorney permission to argue for a change of venue after jury selection but before the jury was sworn in. The ACLU attorney Wirin was described by the LATimes as "wearing a new beard he acquired on his recent trip to Red China." He said he was not arguing on behalf of Elizabeth but rather just felt there would be a fairer trial if it was moved out of Ventura County where the case had seen so much press. The D.A. objected, arguing Sullivan could make the case for a change of venue just as effectively as Wirin could. At this point, Sullivan had used 19 of his 20 allowed jury exemptions while the D.A. had used only 2 of his exemptions. Nine more jurors were dismissed on this day due to their disapproval of the death sentence, and Sullivan asked for exemptions for 3 jurors, all of whom expressed prejudice towards Elizabeth, believing her guilty. The judge disallowed one of the prejudiced potential jurors due to the fact that Sullivan had only 1 exemption left, but kept the other two. At the end of day 4, the jury pool consisted of 7 men and 5 women, and Sullivan had one last exemption he could use. One juror had to be let go as he was reportedly friends with one of the two men Elizabeth hired to kill Olga.

Elizabeth said the she and Frank had been receiving threatening letters in the mail. She showed a newspaper clipping with a photo of her and her son and over the photo, in red ink, it said things like "hope you hang," "apron strings," "mamma's boy," and "cutthroat." She also showed reporters a letter supposedly from San Francisco that said Olga was a good person and she and her baby had been brutally murdered and the author of the letter then said they hoped the murderer would be executed. Frank also objected in court to his phone bills being opened by the D.A. before being given to him, to which the D.A. apologized for the "mistake."

On Feb. 20, 1959, jury selection was final. The jury ended up being composed of 8 women and 4 men. The petition for a change of venue was also denied by the judge upon the completion of the jury selection, since the reason for change of venue was supposedly the inability to get a jury. In the end, Sullivan used all 20 of his challenges to jurors but still had to settle for three jurors who said they believed Elizabeth was guilty of the crime before the trial began. Elizabeth told the press she did not think she was going to get a fair trial.

Elizabeth was sent to Camarillo Hospital again on Feb. 22, 1959 to undergo a brain wave test. Her attorney in the case, S. Ward Sullivan, sent her to Camarillo trying to prove she had lingering brain trauma from an auto accident a few years prior. She was taken to the County Jail for holding, waiting upon results from the Camarillo's tests.

On Feb. 24, 1959, Elizabeth's trial began. The Times reported she got tears in her eyes when one of the witnesses mentioned Elizabeth's 15 year old daughter Patsy's death in 1948. Elizabeth then got angry when the same witness, Mrs. Reed, testified that Elizabeth wanted her to throw acid in Olga's face and throw her over a cliff. Elizabeth then reportedly laughed when Reed said Elizabeth said she would drug her son during the time of the murder. Elizabeth reported was holding a rosary her son gave her and wearing a diamond necklace her last husband had given her which she called a good luck charm.

Reed testified she had known Elizabeth about 10 years, since they were neighbors in Ventura and Reed was close friends with her daughter Patsy. Reed testified she happened to run into Elizabeth in early 1958 at a bus stop in Santa Barbara then received a phone call from her in the summer of 1958. She then went to Elizabeth's apartment at her request and spoke with her in her bedroom. Reed testified that Elizabeth said there was a woman chasing her son and trying to ruin his career. Elizabeth told Reed that Olga had "gotten herself pregnant" and was then trying to "frame" her son. Reed testified about the acid in face and over the cliff plot and said Elizabeth said it was simple to do, and she had done it before. Reed said Elizabeth offered her $1000 for the job. Reed told Frank about his mother's plots against Olga.

Dorothy Barnett, Frank and Olga's landlady took the stand. She said 2 weeks after the couple moved in, Elizabeth showed up and demanded entry into the couple's apt. Dorothy said she let Elizabeth inside the apt., and the first thing Elizabeth did was run inside to a closet, opening it in haste. She threw open the closet and proclaimed his clothing was not in the closet and that they were not married. Elizabeth then insisted the couple's marriage had been annulled, that her son was living in sin, and that she would kill Olga.

Mary Ann Dowhower testified that in April to June 1957, before Olga had even left Canada for the U.S. (Olga came to the U.S. in Nov. 1957), Elizabeth was saying she suspected her son was dating, and wanted Mary Ann to go to Lover's Lanes in town looking for her son. Dowhower said Elizabeth referred to "Frankie" as a "mama's boy" and said Elizabeth said if he was dating someone, she would "get rid of her."

D.A. Gustafson said that Elizabeth found out about Frank and Olga's relationship in Spring 1958. Frank and his mother argued about him getting married, and so he and Olga married secretly in June 20, 1958, but his mother found out about it the same day.

Ralph Winterstein pled guilty to the crimes of posing as Frank for the fake annulment proceedings with Elizabeth and was in the courtroom as a witness against Elizabeth. On Feb. 25, 1959, he testified that Elizabeth was saying she did not want Olga riding in her son's car and said she was angry at her. Elizabeth asked Ralph to marry her, but Ralph declined. He said she had some fantastic story about how if he married her she would get money and he could have $50,000 but he felt there was something fishy about it. Elizabeth had hired Ralph for a few odd jobs form the Salvation Army, and finally she offered him $100 on August 7, 1958, to pose as Frank with her at a false annulment hearing, where she would pose as Olga. He accepted the offer. He said he only received $34 from Elizabeth for the job and had pled guilty, at that point, to charges of perjury.

On Feb. 25, another witness, Rebecca Diaz, also testified that on Oct. 13, Elizabeth tried to pay her to "get her daughter in law out of town." Diaz said a month later Elizabeth called her and told her to forget the offer, that her services were not needed and it was "today or never." It is assumed this was the point that Elizabeth had hired Moya and Baldonado. Diaz said she met Elizabeth at Mrs. Short's apt. and that Elizabeth told her that a nurse had married her son, was threatening her and demanding large sums of money. Olga had asked for $500 just that day, she said. She said she wanted someone to get the nurse out of town so she would quit harassing her. Elizabeth said Olga used to be married to her son but was not married to him any longer.

She said she did not want this woman ruining her son's career as a lawyer and said she wanted to kill her. Diaz asked Elizabeth why she had not just gone to the police. Elizabeth said that since she had no proof, police would not help. Diaz said she was not interested but Elizabeth called her and asked her if she knew anyone who could do the job if she was not interested later.

At trial, the attorney who gave the annulment to Frank and Olga under fraud by Elizabeth and Ralph, testified he was only paid half the fee and sent the bill to Olga's apartment as he thought Elizabeth was Olga. He said he found out it had been a fraud on Oct. 14, after a call from a Santa Barbara lawyer. He then called Frank, whom he said expressed "shock and surprise."

On Feb. 27, Mrs. Short testified that Frank Duncan called his mother Elizabeth "doll" and promised constantly that he would never leave her. There was a short skirmish in the courtroom between the D.A. and Elizabeth's attorney, Sullivan, over the D.A.'s continuing use of "Frankie" to refer to the grown man "Frank." The judge overruled Sullivan's complaint. The D.A. then asked Mrs. Short about the sleeping arrangements in the 2 bedroom apt. that Elizabeth and Frankie shared before he married Olga. Mrs. Short said Elizabeth's bedroom could be seen from the living room, and one day, she was in the apartment, and Frank was on Elizabeth's bed, visible from the living room, and Elizabeth said to Mrs. Short, "Isn't he beautiful?" Mrs. Short also testified that Elizabeth said that Frank had "come home to his mother" on the night of his marriage. Short said that Elizabeth said to Frank every day that if he did not get an annulment, she would get one for him, that she had done it before and would do it again. Short testified that a week after the false annulment, Frank tore up the annulment papers in front of his mother saying they were not worth the paper they were written on, although Frank had testified to the Grand Jury that he did not know of the annulment until two months later when the attorney informed him of the annulment. Mrs. Short said over the last two years, she had witnessed Elizabeth try to ruin her son's marriage, and try to buy murder accomplices from at least half a dozen people. She said Elizabeth created elaborate schemes to try to murder Olga.

Short said Elizabeth said she would kill Olga and Frank as she would rather see Frank dead than living with Olga. Short testified that Elizabeth had suggested someone tie Frank up with rope, drug him and put him to bed for a few days to "stop this nonsense." Another time Short said Elizabeth talked to Reed about kidnapping Frank and taking him to San Francisco. Short said Olga had given a wallet to Frank for his birthday but Elizabeth had cut it into pieces, and Short saved the pieces and exhibited them in the courtroom. Three days after Elizabeth cut up the wallet, it was announced in the news that Olga was missing, to which Elizabeth said "she's gone by this time." Short said Elizabeth was looking for a way out of paying the hit men and so she came up with this blackmailing idea, told her son and he told authorities. When Mrs. Short stepped down from the witness stand for recess, Elizabeth stood up and screamed "you're a liar" but was subdued by her attorney. Duncan continued, screaming, "this woman has my clothes on right now and she's a liar! I feel like tearing them right off her!"

Mrs. Esquivel took the stand on Feb. 27. This witness was the one who introduced Duncan to the two men who killed Olga for pay. Esquivel testified that Short and Duncan came into her café asking if she knew anyone who could help get rid of someone. Esquivel said she set up the meeting between Moya and Baldonado and overheard Elizabeth telling the men she would pay them $3000, that she had acid and sleeping pills, that she had a car if they needed one and she would go with them if they needed her to. She said early in the morning on Nov. 18, she found Moya and Baldonado in the bathroom of her home with blood on their clothing. On Nov. 21, Esquivel went to see Duncan at a different café on request of Moya and Baldonado. Esquivel said Elizabeth said she did not have the money she owed "the boys" but felt she was being watched by police, and had a check from her son she was going to cash and give the money to "the boys." Esquivel told her she needed to work it out with the boys as she was not involved.

Esquivel said she was taken to the police station on Dec. 4, and saw Frank Duncan there. Duncan then told her that she was blackmailing his mother and if she did it again, he would scalp her. Defense attorney Sullivan questioned Esquivel as to her part in this since she knew what was going on. Esquivel hesitated several times upon answering and said she was not sure exactly what was going on and was not involved.

On March 3, 1959, Julia Ellen Price, a 48 year convict in Corona Women's Prison, who was in County jail with Elizabeth earlier in the year, testified that Elizabeth had a plan to escape from the County jail on Jan. 10, 1959. She said

Elizabeth told her she was going to ask for medication after the shift change at midnight and when the guard came in, she planned to "kill her, throw her in a cell and take her keys." Price identified Mildred Wolfe as the attendant Elizabeth planned to kill and then Price said she tipped off authorities to the planned escape. Price also said Elizabeth said that her daughter-in-law got what she deserved and that the two men she hired to murder Olga were stupid to not get their pay from her up front. Another woman, Gladys Ruth Kline, age 24, had shared a jail cell with Elizabeth in the County jail and recounted the escape plot for the jury as well. As Kline began to tell about the escape plot, Baldonado, one of the paid murderers, jumped up in his seat yelling he could not take anymore, demanding to be removed from the courtroom. He was there, from jail, as a possible witness. He was removed from the courtroom to a nearby room and said to relax after smoking a cigarette.

Kline continued to testify that Elizabeth offered her $2,000 to help her escape from the County jail in January 1959. Kline said Elizabeth asked her if she knew how the cell doors worked and said she could get one of the guards in her cell as Kline got the other guard in her own cell, and they would "do something" to them. Kline said Elizabeth warned her not to tell anyone for she had connections on the outside who would harm her, even if Elizabeth stayed in jail and Kline was released. Kline said Elizabeth claimed to know which key worked the elevators and said she knew someone a few blocks from the jail who could transport them to Hollywood once they escaped. Kline said Elizabeth said she knew a doctor who could change her identity, including her fingerprints. Kline said the idea of an escape seemed foolish and impractical. The District Attorney introduced notes from the jail guards about Elizabeth's escape plot, which was signed by Kline. Kline also said that Elizabeth denied having anything to do with Olga's death and claimed she was being blackmailed, although she spoke of Olga in negative terms calling her a Russian spy, a drug addict, etc. Kline said Elizabeth said she loved her son very much and remarked how it is surprising to what lengths a mother will go if she does not approve of the person her son marries.

Another cell mate during her stay in County jail, Barbara Edwards, aged 35, testified that Elizabeth had commented that Baldonado and Moya had beat Olga repeatedly and she just would not die, making derogatory remarks about her not dying easily. Edwards also said Elizabeth told her her best bet was to use the insanity plea to get out of the murder charges, and then instructed Edwards on how to "fool" psychiatrists.

On March 4, 1959, Elizabeth testified on the stand that she had plotted to tie her son up and kidnap him, but denied ever plotting to do harm to Olga. Elizabeth admitted saying she wanted to tie up her son and kidnap him after he was married. She testified she said that in her apartment, in front of Mrs. Short, Mrs. Reed, and Mrs. Helen Franklin, who had been subpoenaed to court but had not yet shown. Elizabeth testified that she said "Frankie had just flipped his lid" and she said she called her sister in Los Angeles and asked her to get an apartment for her. Elizabeth said she was going to tie up "Frankie," who was 30 years old at the time, and still living with his mother though married to Olga, and take him to this apartment once he fell asleep. When asked what she would do with him there, she said she just didn't want to "lose" him and said she would just talk to him for a few days there. When asked by her attorney on the stand if she ever told her son of this plan, she said that she would have to be out of her mind to ever tell him she had considered such a thing. When asked if she discussed kidnapping Olga at any time, she said no, that she was only interested in kidnapping her son.

Elizabeth testified that she had taken an overdose of sleeping pills in November 1957 after a conflict with "Frankie," and that she bought a gun after he got married in June 1958, to use to kill herself. Elizabeth said she had been relying on sleeping pills for the last 10 years due to her daughter's sudden death. She got teary at this point and said she had about 1500 sleeping pills in her apt. at the time she overdosed on them in Nov. 1957. Elizabeth said the conflict in Nov. that caused the sleeping pill overdose was over Elizabeth being married to a man, Leonard Sollene, 3 months prior, and her refusing to live with him and instead insisting on living with "Frankie," her adult son while Leonard lived with his own mother. Elizabeth was asked to sign annulment papers, refused, but an annulment was granted anyway which angered her. Elizabeth said Frank told her to move out so she wrote a suicide note to her mother, and another to Frank, then took the sleeping pills and got into bed. She went on to boast it takes a brave person to attempt suicide and said if she had to live alone, she did not want to live. She said she was put into Cottage Hospital in Santa Barbara for a week for the overdose but denies meeting Olga there as a nurse who attended to her.

Elizabeth claimed she first met Olga in April 1958, when her son introduced her as a nurse that had helped her at Cottage Hospital. She said she did not know the nurse's name, did nothing to break up their romance and never made threats against Olga later. Elizabeth claims she did not try to break up their romance, claiming she did not know about it, or their wedding, until the day before the wedding, on June 19, 1958. Elizabeth said Frank made some kind of comment about marrying a nurse in July and she said she told him he couldn't afford to get married right then, that they had just gotten a new place to live, and thousands of dollars of furniture. She said she was sick and could not work, and said that on June 19, Frank promised her he would not get married. Frank told Elizabeth the name of this nurse he planned to marry that night, and Elizabeth immediately looked her up in the phone book and called her. She said she told Olga that she did not like that Frank was only coming home every other night and that she wanted her son to marry someone who was virtuous, not like Olga, and she also said she wanted him marrying someone who liked her and would visit her. Olga then swore at Elizabeth and told her she would marry Frank regardless of how Elizabeth felt. Elizabeth then said she called her a foreigner and said she was mad.

Elizabeth said that Frank did not come home on June 20, and she suspected they got married. On June 21, Elizabeth talked to one of Olga's neighbors and one of the nurses she worked with to confirm the marriage to Frank. Elizabeth said that upon returning from Olga's apt. to confirm the marriage from her neighbor, Frank was home, and she asked him if he had gotten married. He said he had and she asked why he did so when he promised he wouldn't and then he refused to talk about it anymore. She said he then left, but returned again that night. A week later, Elizabeth said she went to Olga's apt., found her with Frank, and an argument began. Elizabeth said she told Olga she did not want her married to her son and Olga told her to get out of their house. Elizabeth said at that point, Frank took her for a ride and then home. Elizabeth denied Frank ever called her "doll" as Mrs. Short had testified and said he only called her "mom" or "mother." Elizabeth went on to testify that in August or September, she went to Olga's landlady and tried to convince her that the two were not married. She got the landlady to let her into their apt. and showed the landlady that Frank's clothes were not in the closet. Elizabeth denies making any threats about Olga at this point, and also denies saying they were living in sin.

Elizabeth was reportedly calm throughout her testimony, but for two times. One time was when she spoke of her deceased daughter Patsy, who died ten years prior at the age of 14, and the second time when explaining how much she wanted her son to return home to her after he got married. Elizabeth said she was mad at Olga for marrying her son. Elizabeth admitted meeting with the prosecution's witnesses against her, but denied talking to them about the murder plots they all said occurred. Elizabeth said she was being blackmailed by Baldonado and Moya and that she paid them $355 over three separate meetings as she feared they would kill her and her son. Elizabeth then expounded on her blackmail concept, saying she was pulled into Esquivel's café by Moya, who said Esquivel's husband was angry at the legal representation he received from her son Frank and that he wanted his money back ($500) or she and Frank would be killed. Elizabeth said the men made her pawn one of her rings for $175 that day she was "pulled into" the café, and she said another time she was forced to cash a check from her son to pay her bills and give the men $150. She said she gave them $10 another time. She claimed to not tell Frank right away because she was afraid he would go down to the café and get hurt as the people at the café were thuggish. Elizabeth said eventually Frank found out she had paid the men and they reported it to the police that night. Elizabeth was shown a line-up of men to identify the men who were blackmailing her, and Moya was in that line up. She did not identify him. Later, Elizabeth was taken into a room with Moya alone, and she said she recognized him but still did not identify him as one of the blackmailers because she was "not for putting people in jail." She said that Frank then threatened to leave her home, which he lived in with his mother, if she did not identify the men. So she then identified Moya, saying she felt sorry for him. Elizabeth denied ever discussing Olga or any murder plots with Baldonado, Moya or Esquivel.

When asked about the Romeros who had testified against her, Elizabeth said that the wife been in a fight with her husband Rudy, and had on bandages and had said she had tried to slit her wrists. Elizabeth said she gave her $20 for rent which they needed. She denied paying them for any other reason and said she could not have offered them $1000 or more to kill Olga as she did not have that kind of money to give.

On March 5, 1959, Elizabeth went back on the stand. The D.A. was said to have investigated "11 of 16 known or purported marriages" and her 6 children on this day. Elizabeth acknowledged 10 of the marriages, but said she had no knowledge of the 11th, and she also had previously claimed to only having 2 children, Frank and her deceased daughter Patsy. Over objections from her attorney, Elizabeth was questioned by the D.A. about her relationship with her son Frank. Elizabeth said she loved Frank and was devoted to him. The D.A. asked if she loved Frank more than her other children and she said yes. She then tried to refute having six children. Elizabeth finally admitted to having 6 children while the D.A. said he believes in actuality she had 7 children.

The D.A. began to explore Elizabeth's many marriages. When asked about her marriage in 1927 to Edward Lynchberg, she said she didn't remember him. She said her first husband was Dewey Tessier whom she married at the age of 15, and she said it was a "Mexican divorce" and she never saw the papers. She said she had 3 children from Tessier: Dewey, jr. who was in the Air Force in Monterrey, Mexico, Hazel of Dallas, and Dorothy of Abilene, Texas. The D.A. said her other husband, Mr. Mitchell, was still married to her when she was married to Tessier, and she said Mitchell had gotten a divorce in Silver City, N.M. The D.A. said Elizabeth married Frank Low in Los Angeles on July 13, 1928, and Frank, her son, was borne about 4 months later, in Nov. 1928 (thus she was already 5 months pregnant when they married). Elizabeth then married Frank Duncan on April 24, 1932, and her son Frank took his last name. Elizabeth had one daughter named Patsy with Frank, Sr., but she died in her teens in 1948. Frank Duncan got an annulment of the marriage, claiming that Elizabeth was still married to Frank Low. Duncan admitted she received the annulment papers but did not answer and allowed a default judgment, saying she was not married to Low at the time and was "not interested" in the annulment hearing.

The D.A. caught Elizabeth in her lies when he asked her if she had not told Frank about the money she had paid her supposed blackmailer on Nov. 13, until Nov. 22, because Olga was missing and she did not want to upset him more. Elizabeth said yes, that was the reason for the delay. But the D.A. then said Olga did not disappear until Nov. 17, so how could that make sense? Elizabeth acted confused and got in some odd verbal skirmishes with the D.A. It was then relayed that Elizabeth reported the blackmail to the police on Nov. 22, yet continued to meet with the alleged blackmailers and continued to give them money after the police report, without reporting such activities to the police involved. Elizabeth said the police gave her a device to use on her phone to record the blackmailers but she did not use it. Elizabeth also said that Baldonado and Moya did not know Olga and had no reason to kill her.

Elizabeth got into fights with the D.A. throughout the trial. At one point, Elizabeth yelled at the D.A. to not stand so close to her, saying also "you better get away," to which the D.A. retorted, "I will," as he walked to the far end of the jury box. Elizabeth then said that was the best place for him and the D.A. eagerly agreed, mocking her violent tendencies, although seemingly unbeknownst to her. At another time, Elizabeth burst out, calling the D.A. a liar, and was admonished by the judge for such an outburst. Elizabeth continued to claim she never wanted Olga killed and began to cry on the stand, saying she would never want someone killed as she knew the pain of her own daughter dying.

On March 6, 1959, Frank Patrick Duncan took the stand as the second defense witness, following three days of his mother's testimony at her own trial. Frank said he was proud that he had lived with his mother almost his entire life, saying this at age 30, and said he had dated "many, many" women and that his mother encouraged it. He said he had asked one woman to marry him prior, but she had turned him down. Frank testified that his mother had been taking 8-12 sleeping pills a day for the last 10 years, since the death of Patsy, her daughter. He said she tried to overdose on sleeping pills on Nov. 6, 1957, due to a misunderstanding he had had with his mother about her own annulment papers. He said he began dating Olga after the hospitalization, where he met her, and did not tell his mother he was planning to marry Olga as his mother was "petrified" of being alone and he did not want to hurt her. He said he promised to her the night before his marriage he would not marry Olga, but then he did marry her, returning to Elizabeth at 10 AM the next morning. Frank said his mother was uncontrollable and in a panic when he arrived. Frank said his mother did not like Olga, but he hoped once their baby was borne, Elizabeth would warm up to her. He denied Elizabeth ever threatening Olga.

Frank testified that in late summer of 1958, Mrs. Reed came to him saying his mother was plotting to harm Olga. Frank confronted Elizabeth who said she was not trying to harm Olga, but just said she was going to tie Frank up and kidnap him. Frank said he was angry upon hearing this and thought it sounded idiotic and childish. Frank said he last saw his wife on Nov. 8, 1958, 10 days before she went missing. He said he left their home at approx. 1 AM. He said they had an affectionate marriage, though he did not speak to her in the 10 days prior to her going missing.

On March 9, 1959, applause erupted in Judge Blackstock's courtroom when he denied a motion for a mistrial and the applause was noted in the court records on March 10, 1958.

On March 10, 1959, Elizabeth's murder trial resumed with Valentine Ponomaroff on the stand. Ponomaroff was an insurance salesman in Santa Barbara and was friends with Olga and Frank. He met them in late Nov. 1957, and said they met in a Santa Barbara hotel where Frank introduced Olga as his date. In June 1958, just before they were married, Pomonaroff said that Frank said Olga was getting too serious and he wished he could pawn her off on someone else. On August 15, 1958, two days after Frank bought an insurance policy from him, Pomonaroff said he got a call from Elizabeth, asking he come to her apt. When he arrived, Elizabeth wanted to know who the beneficiary was on the $29,462 policy Frank had bought days prior. When he said he could not divulge such information due to confidentiality issues, she produced a copy of the insurance policy, pointing out that executors and administrators were assigned to carry out the beneficiary benefits. She then said Frank did not have a will, thus executors, etc. did not exist. Pomonaroff said Frank was an attorney and knew what he was doing.

Upon further inspection of the form, Elizabeth exclaimed, "so that's where she lives" upon seeing Olga's address, and followed with negatives statements about Olga being a foreigner, saying she left a husband and two kids, and saying that Frank and Olga are not really married, producing the falsified annulment papers. Elizabeth told Pomonaroff twice not to tell Frank about their conversation that day. Pomonaroff testified he immediately went to Frank and told him about the annulment papers his mother produced and also said that she knew where Olga lived. This is important as Frank said he did not learn of the false annulment papers his mother filed until August 1958. Pomonaroff was implying that Frank knew of the false annulment in June, due to him telling Frank himself. Pomonaroff testified that Frank immediately called Olga once contacted by him and told her to wait at her apt., saying he needed to talk to his mother and Olga to "straighten things out." A week later, Pomonaroff said to Frank he should be living with his wife not his mother, to which Frank replied "you don't know my mother."

A witness who had been subpoenaed and was missing, but finally appeared, Helen Franklin, age 69, testified on Mar. 10, 1959. She said that Elizabeth had said she did not like Olga and did not want her to marry Frank. After Olga and Frank were married, Franklin said Elizabeth asked her and Mrs. Short to give Frank sleeping pills and tie him up. She said there was rope in the bathroom for the deed but that Frank did not want to take the pills so the plan fell through. On cross-examination, Franklin clarified that Elizabeth said she tried to give sleeping pills to Frank but he would not take them, but denied hiding in a closet waiting for Frank as Mrs. Short had testified. Franklin said she went home to San Francisco and that Elizabeth called her repeatedly to "do some sewing." Elizabeth knew Franklin owed some bills and threatened to tell bill collectors where Franklin was if she did not help her. Franklin said she saw Elizabeth in San Francisco sometime between Dec. 5 and Dec 11, which was 3 weeks after Olga went missing and 2 weeks before her body was found. Franklin said Elizabeth said Olga had gone away, she thought to Mexico, and was glad she was gone.

On March 10, 1959, another witness on the stand was Sara Contreras, who owned the car that was later linked to Olga's disappearance. She supposedly "rented" her car to Baldonado and Moya on Nov. 13. On Nov. 14, records proved that Frank talked to Mrs. Esquivel's husband's probation officer, and Frank testified that on that day, he also told Mrs. Esquivel's husband he was going back to jail. The timing of this being one day after the kidnapping of Olga had begun seemed odd.

Another witness on the stand on March 10, was a Santa Barbara telephone operator who testified that Elizabeth called and asked for Olga's unlisted number. She remembered the call as Elizabeth said she was a relative of Olga's but could not spell her maiden name, Kupezyk, which seemed off if they were relatives. She said Elizabeth was very insistent and even said "we have to put a stop to this Olga."

On March 10, a Santa Barbara Police officer testified that Frank told him on Nov. 24, 1958, that his mother may be involved with his wife's disappearance, and there may be some connection with her claim of being blackmailed. Another Santa Barbara Police officer testified that on Dec. 13, he brought Mrs. Short and Elizabeth together, face to face, at the police station. He said Elizabeth told Mrs. Short not to take a lie detector test until she had an attorney and asked her "why she did it." Mrs. Short replied that she just wanted to "tell the truth."

Mrs. Esquivel was brought to the stand, and forced to finally admit that she was testifying against Elizabeth because she was told she could become a defendant in the case for hooking up Elizabeth with the two murderers at her café, and if she testified, charges would not be brought against her. A past physician of Elizabeth's, who treated her after her 1957 drug overdose, testified that he asked her why she tried to kill herself. She said she was afraid her son was going to leave her. The doctor said her son was a grown man, and was going to get married and leave her at some point, so what would she do then. The doctor said she said that Frank would not "dare" get married. A Santa Barbara store operator, Genevieve Miller, said that Elizabeth made contact with her 2 days after Frank and Olga got married, warning her of bills Olga was charging to Frank and Olga's account, and recalled Elizabeth saying repeatedly that Frank would never live with Olga.

Patricia Hamilton, Olga's landlady after she got married, said two days after the marriage, Elizabeth showed up at her apt. and a loud fight with yelling erupted. Frank reportedly told his mother to "shut up," and Olga was crying. Frank left with his mother when she stomped her foot down and demanded that Frank was going home with her, which he did. The wife of a Santa Barbara insurance agent, Evelyn Hope Clarke, testified that Elizabeth called on Nov. 12, trying to change the beneficiary on her son's insurance policy. She said Frank was getting an annulment and that Olga was causing a lot of problems.

Santa Barbara attorney Charles Lynch testified that Elizabeth came to his office on Aug. 11, 1958, saying her son had gotten married and would no longer support her. She asked the attorney to talk to Frank and ask him for money, also adding Frank was angry with her. Lynch said he was old enough to be married and make his own choices but Elizabeth insisted Olga was not the right girl for Frank, said she was older, had a few kids, and was trying to keep Frank from Elizabeth. Lynch said he talked to Frank around Sept. 12,

1958, and that Frank was angry that Lynch had revealed the false annulment papers existed. Lynch argued he had not breached confidentiality and Frank said he would have covered it up if he could have.

A Santa Barbara Superior Court reporter and bailiff reported seeing Elizabeth in a courtroom in Fall 1958 with Diane and Rudy Romero. Elizabeth was reportedly sitting between the two, with her arms around them both, with her head on Diane's shoulder. Both of the Romeros have testified that Elizabeth tried to get them to kill Olga.

Pictures of the courthouse on March 11, 1959 in Ventura show a county guard holding back a flood of laughing and smiling women who were all trying to get seats for the Duncan murder trial as spectators.

On Friday, March 13, 1959, testimony ended in the murder trial and the jury would begin deliberating the following Monday. Elizabeth reportedly complained about two women in the audience "grimacing" at her at trial, but was described as "chipper and smiling" as she was led back to jail after the testimonies. When the press asked Elizabeth how she was feeling now that all the evidence had been presented to the jury, she said she did not know how to answer and hoped everything was "alright." In his last statements to the jury, the D.A. stated that the two who committed the murder, Moya and Baldonado, would probably get the electric chair and it would be unfair for Elizabeth to just walk free. The D.A. also condemned Frank for not taking proper measures to insure the safety of Olga, and said it was due to his insistence that the "blackmail" crime be reported that really broke the case wide open. He also said the defense's theories in this case were "fantastic, weird, and unbelievable." The D.A. argued that Olga's marriage certificate turned out to be her death certificate and argued for a sentence of guilty of first-degree murder charges for Elizabeth. The D.A. also argued the motive was intense hatred of Olga and intense love of her son, Frank and said this could have been any girl who walked into this situation and that this could have happened to any of the jury's sisters or daughters. The D.A. also argued that at least Baldonado and Moya admitted their crimes, whereas Elizabeth continued to deny hers. As the D.A. scolded both Elizabeth and Frank in his closing arguments, Elizabeth hurled an epithet, verbally audible, at him and even rose from her chair, being held back by court deputies, when she said it.

People in the courtroom said she called him an "S.O.B" while Elizabeth says she called him a liar, to which the D.A. retorted, "excuse me?"

The D.A. referred to Frank as a "spineless jellyfish," saying if anyone knew his mother committed this crime, it was him. He also asked if Frank was a man or a mouse. He expressed pity for Frank, saying he was a product of Elizabeth's domination, but said that did not excuse him for going on the witness stand in this trial to defend his mother. He commented that neither Elizabeth nor Frank seem to display any genuine loss over Olga's death and both smile for cameras. The D.A. asked the jury if they had ever seen anyone so seemingly giddy at a murder trial and said Elizabeth only shows she is glad Olga is gone. The D.A. also said that Frank was on a date with a woman on Dec. 10, 1958, just after he found out Olga was killed.

During the defense's closing arguments, Sullivan interjected a new slant on things, saying perhaps Elizabeth was caught in a kidnapping for ransom plot against her will. Elizabeth's attorney argued perhaps Moya and Baldonado were helping Mrs. Esquivel retrieve the $500 paid for her husband's legal fees to Frank, and then they decided to kidnap Olga and hold her for ransom to get their $500. But then Olga fought, and they killed her, rather than just keeping her for ransom, and they did not mean to kill her, but now instead of a kidnap for ransom, they had a murder on their hands. The defense then said the would-be kidnappers could not go to Frank for the money because he was an attorney and they had just committed murder, but they were able to go after Elizabeth. The defense argued Moya would not have committed a murder for just $175 and said the reason Elizabeth did not identify Moya at first in the line-up was because Baldonado was still free and she feared he would harm her if she identified Moya. Elizabeth's lawyer argued Baldonado and Moya were trying to pawn their botched kidnapping gone wrong, now murder, on Elizabeth to save themselves and had nothing to lose in doing so. The defense attorney argued Elizabeth was an easy target as she did not like Olga and did not approve of her marriage to her son.

The defense attorney argued that Frank was "weak" and "dominated" by his mother most of his life, and also said Olga was "erratic, impetuous and testy," as seen in court, but he said such behaviors did not indicate guilt. Defense argued Elizabeth could have taken the Fifth, not testifying on the grounds of self-incrimination, but she wanted to testify to clear her name. He also said many of the witnesses in the case could be considered accomplices and charged with crimes and thus there was a question as to the veracity of their claims, such as was the case with Mrs. Esquivel. The defense also argued that there is nothing wrong with a mother loving her son, and that she had said she loved Frank more than her other 6 children, thus his situation was of more importance to her.

On March 16, 1959, the jury, after deliberating a little under 3 hours, found Elizabeth guilty of first degree murder. Upon hearing the verdict, she turned to Frank and told him not to worry too much. Later in jail, she reportedly broke down to her attorney, crying, saying she did not think the jury would return with a guilty verdict, saying she did not think they would do that "to her." Elizabeth was calm and smiling before and after the verdict, while Frank was visibly shaken during the reading of the verdict. Later he said he knew it was coming. The following day Elizabeth would be back in court for the jury to hear testimony to decide whether she should get the electric chair, aka the death penalty, or life in prison. Following the sentencing hearing was scheduled a hearing regarding her plea of innocence by reason of insanity.

On March 17, 1959, the sentencing hearing for Elizabeth began, in which the prosecution argued for the death penalty. Several shady chapters of Elizabeth's life came out at this hearing. The San Francisco Police Department testified that Elizabeth was convicted of running a house of prostitution in San Francisco in 1953 under the name of Betty Cogbill. She was sentenced to 30 days in jail and a year of probation. In 1957, Elizabeth tried to have an illegal abortion performed for a girl in San Francisco, telling a doctor her husband had gotten the girl pregnant, but the doctor said he knew Elizabeth was not married and said he would have no part of it. Later, she tried to pay the same girl $500 to testify for her in an annulment hearing. This gal was called to testify and she said that they did go to the doctor for an abortion and that she had been having sex with Elizabeth's last husband, whom she would later have an annulment with. This last husband, in a long line of husbands, in 1957, was promised a split of $200,000 for marrying her. She squatted in a house in Santa Barbara for several months in 1946, saying she would buy the house then not buying it, and she had Frank run the owners off the property, when he was in his mid-teens, with a rifle. In 1948, she wrote a bad check under a fake name and said her husband was a Navy doctor to get a loan for a car she bought and never repaid. She had three "romantic interludes" in hotels with a "bus driver" in 1956, then sued him for alimony, even though they had never been married, though she insisted they were, and she also said he left her pregnant. She proposed to a man in 1947, he refused, she used his last name later on an application for a beer license. In 1933, she was sued for annulment based on bigamy. The prosecutor argued he was showing this evidence to display a pattern of fraud and also to show she has committed many crimes for which she was never punished.

On March 18, 1959, the prosecutor gave more evidence of Elizabeth's shady past. Reports of this day say the prosecutor told the jury about Elizabeth proposing marriage to one of her son's friends in law school, Stephen Gillis, offering him $50,000 to marry her in Jan. 1954, and later claiming she had a child by him. Elizabeth then took a pregnant woman to the doctor under a false name, using the last name of Gillis, then used the pregnancy paperwork in court against Gillis for child support and alimony. Elizabeth gave Gillis a bad check for $10,000 and also testified against Gillis in a State Bar hearing, saying he made her pregnant, preventing him from sitting for the Bar Exam after finishing law school. Gillis said the marriage was arranged by phone and was supposed to just last a year or two. In Spring of 1955, Gillis said he received annulment papers from Elizabeth, and filed them, but in Dec. 1955, the annulment was denied when Elizabeth then said she was pregnant from the marriage. In March 1956, at an annulment hearing, Gillis saw the doctor's records saying Elizabeth was pregnant (though that too was a fraud) and he said the marriage was legally annulled on April 5, 1956. Gillis got out of the Marine Corps in July 1956 and applied to take the Bar Exam. He was told he could not sit for the Bar because of allegations Elizabeth had made and her testimony before the Bar on May 16, 1958.

It was also exposed that Elizabeth wrote a $50,000 personal check in 1952 as a down payment on a $255,000 apartment house with only $29 in her bank account. In 1951, she got a businessman, George Satriano, in San Francisco, to marry her on the spur of the moment with her usual promises of wealth, had him support her for several months, got him to trade his car in for a Cadillac and then she took possession of it instead of alimony payments. Satriano testified that Frank and his mother hid his Cadillac from him several times, one time even prompting him to call the police over it being stolen. Elizabeth was later recorded by a private investigator, offering him $500 to throw acid in Satriano's face. Satriano said he feared for his life after hearing the recording of her offering to pay for acid in his face, and said he would run home from work at night in fear, as she was hanging out around his shop. He said he finally got divorce papers in July 1953.

While Satriano was on the stand, Elizabeth was asked if she was attracted to Satriano. She replied that she was attracted to him in the past and still was attracted to him. She said she never offered anyone money to throw acid in his face and that they had a tumultuous marriage. Apparently Satriano's "glib" responses to questions set the judge, jury, spectators and even Frank and Elizabeth into fits of laughter so hearty that a recess had to be held for everyone to compose themselves after fits of laughter.

On March 19, 1959, Dr. Louis R. Nash, assistant director of Camarillo Hospital, testified at Elizabeth's sentencing hearing that she was not insane. He said she had a "psychopathic personality" and was a "pathological liar." This was a bombshell to the hearing, as this psychiatrist was brought to the stand as a defense witness! The testimony was going to be used to show her fragile emotional state, to help argue against the death penalty, by the defense. Nash testified he had examined Elizabeth on January 8, 12, 17 and 28, and also during the trial on March 4-6. Nash said he had concluded that Elizabeth was a "maladjusted individual, impulsive, egocentric, immature emotionally, unable to stand frustrations, unable to maintain her emotional equilibrium and independence during minor or major stresses." He said she had been problematic to herself and society for many years and thus was a "psychopathic personality." He said a symptom of such a disturbance was "poor judgment" and "unacceptable behavior." The D.A. asked the doctor to clarify as to whether he was saying she was insane or not based on his conclusions shared in the courtroom. Dr. Nash said she was not insane by his calculations. The D.A. asked if most, if not all, criminals fit the category of "psychopathic personality," and the doctor replied that arbitrarily breaking the law is the very definition of this type of behavior. Dr. Nash said a "psychopathic personality" was a "social misfit who uses society as a battleground." The D.A. asked if such a person was confined in an institution, if he would act out the same way, with acts of violence and impulsiveness, and the doctor agreed such behavior would continue inside an institution as well.

COMMITMENT CRITERIA

Dr. Nash said he had not asked Elizabeth how many men she had been sexual with, and said he would not believe her answer anyway. The D.A. asked if that was because she was a pathological liar, and the doctor said that was not the reason, even though she was a pathological liar. He said he would not believe her because she said she was only a social drinker yet fit into a personality type of alcoholics and drug addicts. He said she knew the difference between right and wrong and understood consequences for wrongful acts.

On March 19, 1959, Elizabeth was back on the stand and several times raised her five fingers to indicate she wanted to take the 5th, to not incriminate herself during her testimony about her marriages which numbered at least 10, but perhaps up to 20. The D.A. and Elizabeth "clashed" several times during sentencing hearings, as she could not keep her stories about her past straight, and once it was reported she did not answer a question, stating it was none of the D.A.'s business. She took 5th Amendment privileges when asked if she bore a child from Gillis in 1956, yet when taunted she was no longer of child-bearing age at that time, she retorted that she most certainly had delivered a child from Gillis. The D.A. probed for the name of the hospital and attending doctor at the child's birth and again Elizabeth took the 5th, raising her 5 fingers on the stand. The D.A. continued, saying he interpreted that as her trying to get out of admitting she committed perjury in front of the State Bar committee by testifying she had a child from Gillis to keep him from becoming an attorney. She again raised her 5 fingers, taking the 5th.

Elizabeth testified she could not remember the details of many of her marriages because they did not mean much to her. When asked why she had so many marriages, she said she was looking for something, but said after marrying them, she no longer wanted them. The D.A. said they had brought evidence of 10 marriages into the courtroom and he felt there were more. He asked her if she had more marriages hidden out there that they did not find, and she again took the 5th.

The D.A. asked Elizabeth if her motive in having so many marriages was sex, and she smiled and answered perhaps it was. He then went on to suggest she needed to be married at all times in case she became pregnant from some other man's child. Elizabeth replied that was not so. The D.A. then asked her if she had not been a madame in a prostitution house to put her son through law school. She shouted, "No!" The D.A. probed further, stating that was her occupation at the time, while Elizabeth said it was instead her "position" at the time. When asked again about all of the marriages seeming to run on top of one another, she again took the 5th.

The defense then brought Frank up to the stand, and he said his mother had been an "extremely fine mother" and would choose her again, even after all of this embarrassment. Frank reportedly then looked tenderly at his mother as she wiped away a tear.

On March 20, 1959, the jury delivered a verdict of the death sentence by gas chamber after less than 5 hours of deliberations. Elizabeth complained she got a rotten deal due to a biased jury and said that their request for a change of venue had been wrongfully denied. She was taken back to jail after her sentence was read in court.

Both defense and prosecution agreed to let the judge, rather than the jury, decide the issue of Elizabeth's sanity, based on the testimony of two court-appointed doctors in the case, Dr. Nash and Dr. Phillip May, both from Camarillo State Mental Hospital. Dr. Nash previously testified Elizabeth was sane, and another doctor, Dr. Bielinski, a doctor presented by the defense, testified on March 20 that she was not insane, as well. The D.A. said he saw no areas where an appeal could take hold to overturn the sentencing, yet the defense attorney continued to insist an appeal would take place. Frank also was defiant, saying that an appeal would certainly overturn this court's decisions. The D.A. said to Frank that he was going to the State Bar to flag Frank's behavior to them, which could bring his license to practice law into question by the license granting authorities.

As Elizabeth waited in jail for the sanity hearing, she was on a 24 hour watch, lest she try to commit suicide. The jail staff said the night that the jury gave her the death sentence, after crying in jail to her attorney, she took her usual sleeping pill and went to sleep. The next morning she ate her usual breakfast and complained about the food as usual, reported the Times. The jail staff said she had asked to go to the medical area of jail twice so far, once for heart trouble and another time for food poisoning. While Elizabeth awaited her sanity hearing results, her accomplices who had already admitted guilt, Baldonado and Moya, were awaiting their own sanity and sentencing hearings.

On March 24, 1959, the judge found Elizabeth sane at the time of Olga's plotted murder. A motion was filed by the defense immediately and the hearing to decide if an appeal can be heard was set for April 3, 1959. Later in jail, Elizabeth was in high spirits, expressing faith that she would win an appeal. Frank was also added as co-counsel in his mother's defense on March 24. Part of the grounds for appeal were "new evidence" which the defense admitted it did not yet have. Elizabeth was defiant, saying "they" were not going to "make her cry," and said she had been spending her time in jail reading and playing cards, while also calling the D.A. a "rat."

Also on March 24, another person brought down by Elizabeth had his day in court. Ralph Winterstein, age 26, pleaded guilty to perjury for his part in the bizarre fake annulment hearing that Elizabeth paid for to pretend Olga and Frank were no longer married. The judge sentenced him to 1-14 years in prison. Elizabeth was scheduled to be tried for her part in this annulment fraud, with 4 felony counts, on April 6, which was the day Baldonado was also scheduled for his sanity and sentencing hearing for Olga's murder. Moya's sanity and sentencing hearing was set for April 20.

On April 3, 1959, the judge heard the appeal for a retrial in Elizabeth's case but denied the appeals of Frank and her other attorney, Mr. Sullivan. After the appeal was denied, her defense team argued for life in prison instead of the death penalty but the judge stayed with the death penalty and ordered Elizabeth transferred to the CA Institution for Women in Corona to await the automatic review by the CA Supreme Court. Elizabeth said she welcomed the change of scenery in her move to Corona. The judge also sentenced Elizabeth to 1-14 years of prison for the 4 felony counts associated with her false annulment of Frank and Olga's marriage.

On April 9, 1959, Baldonado, age 25, the man Elizabeth hired to kill Olga, was sentenced to death in the gas chamber. The jury took less than 2 hours to come to their verdict. Baldonado showed no emotion at the reading of his verdict and his hands shook as they were shackled and he was led back to jail. Baldonado's attorney said he would probably appeal for a new trial.

On April 20, Moya's trial began. Both Moya and Baldonado had abandoned their insanity pleas, pled guilty to first-degree murder, and threw themselves on the mercy of the courts. In the courtroom to show support for Moya were his parents from Texas, his 4 siblings and his siblings' children. Moya was eventually sentenced to death in the gas chamber as well.

On June 20, 1959, the LATimes reported the Eavesdrop recording label had produced a "non-fiction story in audio" entitled, "The Duncan Case." The product said it was actual recordings of testimony in Elizabeth's trial, but the sound quality was said to be poor, even incomprehensible at times, and was said to be narrated by a local radio personality.

On Feb. 5, 1960, John Malmin won the CA-NV Associated Press Association picture of the year award for his dramatic photos of the Duncan trial. The winning photo was one that captured Elizabeth's shocked look as she looked at Frank in the courtroom when was found guilty of murder.

On March 11, 1960, the CA Supreme Court upheld and affirmed all three death penalties for Elizabeth, Baldonado and Moya. Moya and Elizabeth appealed for retrials while Baldonado accepted the penalty without appeal. On April 6, 1960, the CA Supreme Court denied appeals for retrials for Moya and Elizabeth after requests by their counsel. Ventura County was cleared to set execution dates for all three at this point. Elizabeth's attorney stated his intent to file a petition with the U.S. Supreme Court at this time. On April 6, the Times reported Moya still had a pending trial asking to be allowed to donate one of his eyes to a blind medical missionary before he died.

On June 3, 1960, ACLU attorney A.L.Wirin filed a petition with the CA Supreme Court, seeking a stay of execution for Elizabeth, Moya and Baldonado, arguing they did not receive fair trials. On June 8, 1960, Wirin's petition for the stay of execution was denied for all 3 defendants. On June 8, Governor Jerry Brown said he had scheduled a clemency hearing for the three in the following week. All three were scheduled to be executed on June 17, 1960. A previous request for a stay of execution was denied by a Ventura judge.

In late May 1961, the U.S. Supreme Court declared there was no reason to retry any of the three defendants in the Duncan murder trials and denied they had not received fair trials. Governor Jerry Brown was then cited as the last hope to overturn the death sentences for the three, with executive clemency, though attorney Wirin said he was considering requesting a rehearing from the U.S. Supreme Court.

In early August 1961, Frank filed a last minute request for a stay of execution, trying to stop his mother's execution which was scheduled for August 16. Frank argued the same things previously argued, that his mother did not receive a fair trial. Previous requests had been denied based on the same criteria. Frank's attempts at saving his mother were futile, as the courts continued to say she received a fair trial. Elizabeth continued to be scheduled for death by gas chamber on Aug. 16, followed by the death of the two men she hired on the same day.

A week before her scheduled death, a judge filed a certificate of probable cause on behalf of Frank and Elizabeth, clearing the way to argue her case before the U.S. Circuit Court of Appeals. During the week that Elizabeth was scheduled to death, the Times reported Frank had been secretly married to his law partner while his mother, whom he was defending, was in jail awaiting the death penalty for murder of his last wife. Frank's new wife, Elinor, confirmed she had married Frank in Carmel on July 25, 1960. Reportedly the couple had visited Elizabeth several times in prison.

In August 1961, both Moya and Baldonado were granted a stay of execution based on paperwork filed by the ACLU attorney Wirin and their deaths were suspended until after Elizabeth's appeals were heard. All three had been scheduled to die in August 1960.

In Jan. 1962, the U.S. Court of Appeals listened to appeals that she did not receive a fair trial. All attempts to prove any of the three received an unfair trial once again failed. In March 1962, Elizabeth filed her second appeal to the U.S. Court of Appeals. This last appeal did not include Baldonado or Moya, and only applied to Elizabeth. In June, 1962, the Court of Appeals once again refused to hear her appeal.

In Aug. 1962, the Times reported Elizabeth was slated to be the 4th woman ever killed in the gas chamber in CA in its 111 year history. Governor Brown said he was appalled at the idea of a woman dying in the gas chamber, but added that did not mean he would stop it. Brown heard appeals from all three of the defendants in the Duncan murder trial but he denied all requests to stay their executions saying he saw no compelling arguments that would facilitate his intervention. At the Governor's clemency hearing, Frank argued for his mother's life, as did Baldonado's mother and Moya's sister. There was some political pressure going on as Richard Nixon was a staunch supporter of the death penalty and was running against Jerry Brown for Governor that Fall, and was saying Brown lacked leadership and condemned his distaste for the death penalty, so Brown felt pressure to not grant a stay of execution to these three. A day before Brown's clemency hearing, an Illinois governor had granted a stay of execution to a death row inmate, commuting the sentence instead to life in prison without parole, which opened the floodgates for other prisoners to ask for clemency as well. Jerry Brown did not want to open such floodgates in CA.

A few hours after Brown denied the stay of execution, the CA Supreme Court also rejected Elizabeth's petition for a retrial based on claims she was drugged by her jailers during the Ventura trials and could not cooperate properly with her lawyer, Mr. Sullivan. The State Supreme Court said this was their final statement about this matter, yet Sullivan said he was petitioning the U.S. Supreme Court on the same grounds as the last two appeals he lost in the CA Supreme Court.

Elizabeth was being prepared to transfer from Corona women's prison to Death Row at San Quentin, and was said to be taking the news that none of her last hour appeals were working and that the Governor had not granted a stay of execution well, but was reported to have said she was "sick and disappointed." She still held out hope that a last minute court appeal was going to save her.

On August 9, 1962, the LATimes ran a photo of a disturbed-looking Frank Duncan, who was pictured leaving the Federal Building in San Francisco, after receiving confirmation that his mother had indeed been executed in the gas chamber at San Quentin at 10:12 AM on August 8. On the day of her execution, Frank, his attorney wife and another attorney were at the courthouse waiting for it to open at 8 AM to file paperwork on Elizabeth's behalf. Frank was told his last plea with the U.S. Court of Appeals had been denied 2 minutes before his mother was walked into the gas chamber at 10 AM.

Elizabeth supposedly told the warden she was innocent as she was led into the death chamber, then asked "where's Frank?" The trio in this murder were the 188th, 189th and 190th prisoners executed by cyanide gas in CA and was the first triple execution since the famous executions of Barbara Graham, Emmett Perkins, and Jack Santo in June 1955. Apparently Barbara Graham asked for a blindfold during her execution. Elizabeth did not ask for a blindfold, but did ask for total sedation before the gassing, which was refused. Elizabeth slept in a cell 14 steps from the gas chamber the night before. She entered the gas chamber, in her prison smock, walking by herself, at 10 AM and approached one of two chairs and sat down, showing no emotion. The chair was big compared to Elizabeth and her feet were said to hang a few feet above the ground as she sat in the chair. Two guards strapped her arms to the chair, as well as placing a belt across her abdomen, then left the room. The Times then detailed a gruesome scene, in far too much detail, of Elizabeth's body convulsing as she died. Fifty-seven people witnessed her death which took approximately 10 minutes, from a glass-encased viewing room in the "apple green" facility. Two witnesses had to be escorted out due to fainting.

The State Warden announced to the press and public that Elizabeth had been executed and it had been a routine execution. He said she slept well the night before, and her last evening meal had been steak, mashed potatoes, peas and coffee and that she had complained about them, as she always did. The warden said she had been given her last rites by the Catholic Church. The warden said she was given Thorazine, "a mild sedative" the night before her execution. He said on the morning of her execution, she also requested Thorazine, saying she wanted it so she would not have to see the people witnessing her execution. She was not given the drugs requested. She was allowed to invite 5 people to watch her execution, which apparently is prison policy but she asked no one to come and wanted no one as a witness. Frank visited her for an hour on the eve before she was executed and she asked to speak to Frank on the morning of her execution but the request was denied. Some in the press doubted she was not under heavy sedation due to Elizabeth's extremely calm manner in the gas chamber but the warden again asserted she was not sedated for the execution. One witness for the execution was the sheriff who got Baldonado to confess and broke the case open, another was the spiritual advisor of Moya, to whom he had confessed. Seven people protested the death sentence outside the prison the night before and day of the executions. Ten minutes before Elizabeth was executed, the stay of executions for Moya and Baldonado were denied as well.

Moya and Baldonado were executed in the gas chamber at San Quentin 3 hours after Elizabeth. Baldonado was said to be brazen and told the warden to be sure to close the door tight and grinned as he was led into the chamber.

Moya entered the gas chamber first, was quickly strapped to a chair and nodded. Both Moya and Baldonado wore white shirts which were open at the neck, dark blue jeans and black shoes. Baldonado came in 15 seconds after Moya, making jokes and laughing. Baldonado had invited his brother and two other family friends to witness his execution, and when he saw them in the witness area, he waved, smiled and told Moya to look at them. Moya turned to look at them, and smiled. Baldonado was strapped in and the two talked in an animated fashion, as well as laughed, shaking their heads and looking at the witnesses who were watching. At 1: 05 PM, the executioner "pulled the lever" and Baldonado saw the lever was down and yelled, "It's down!" so loudly that the witnesses heard him through the glass. The two began to tell each other it was ok, and they were just going to go to sleep. Baldonado mouthed to his brother to take care of his kids for him. At approximately 1:07 PM, it became silent as Baldonado convulsed, looked at Moya, their eyes glazed over and their heads dropped. Moya was said to have died one minute before Baldonado. Baldonado's brother cried while the other two witnesses he invited stared with interest at the events.

The warden said that the night before Moya and Baldonado's executions, they asked for dinners of lobster thermidor, steak, fried oysters, frog legs, and much more, with bicarbonate pills to boot. They did not get frog legs, oysters or lobster, but they did get prime steak and banana cream pie. Baldonado slept his last night from 1:30 AM until 6 AM, when he asked for communion. Moya slept from 1:30 AM until 7:30 AM. As Moya and Baldonado ate, the rest of the prison was on a hunger strike, refusing to eat due to a reduction in recreation time, which was in part caused by Moya and Baldonado. In July, both men had attempted an escape with four other men. The men had smuggled saws into their cells, sawed cell bars off, then held guards hostage until overwhelmed and incapacitated by tear gas.

Frank claimed his mother's body after the execution and it was transported to a San Francisco funeral home for arrangements. Moya's body was donated to science and claimed by Stanford Medical School. Baldonado's body was taken to a Ventura funeral home.

Coincidentally, the same day that Elizabeth was put to death, August 8, Mrs. Short, a key witness in the murder trial, was buried. She had died of a heart attack on August 4, in the Ventura County Hospital.

In June 1966, Frank's second wife, Elinor, was granted a divorce from him based on the grounds of cruelty.

LATimes, Brad Williams, Father Tells Times of Threats, Dec. 16, 1958, p. 1.

LATimes, Gene Blake, Front Page 1 - No Title, Dec. 16, 1958, p. 1.

LATimes. Gene Blake, Mother Gets Bail Reduced in Weird Annulment Case, Dec. 18, 1958, p.2.

LATimes, Gene Blake, Man Who Posed as Mate in Fake Annulment Identified, Dec. 19. 1958, p. 2.

LATimes, Gene Blake, Police Appeal for Help to Find Missing Bride's Body, Dec. 21, 1958, p. A.

LATimes, Gene Blake, Brides Body Found, New Arrests Hinted, Dec. 22, 1958, p. 1.

LATimes, Search Turns Here For Murdered Nurse's Mate, Dec. 24, 1958, p.2.

LATimes, Duncan Case Names Kept From Public, Dec. 25, 1958, p. 2.

LATimes, Husband of Slain Nurse Found Here, Dec. 26, 1958, p. 2.

LATimes, Gene Blake, Case Weighed for 15 Minutes, Dec. 27, 1958, p. 1.

LATimes, Gene Blake, State Organizing Case Against Mrs. Duncan, Dec. 28, 1958, p. 3.

LATimes, Father of Murdered Nurse Meets Son-in-Law Duncan, Dec. 29, 1958, p. 2.

LATimes, Gene Blake, Duncan Plot Story to Jury Disclosed, Dec. 31, 1958, p. 1.

LATimes, Walter Ames, Transcript Tells of Slaying Plan, Dec. 31, 1958, p. 6.

LATimes, Mrs. Duncan Plans to Ask Venue Shift, Jan. 3, 1959, p. B1.

LATimes, Gene Blake, Insanity Plea Made for Mrs. Duncan by Lawyer, Jan. 7, 1959, p. 5.

LATimes, Mrs. Duncan Takes First Sanity Tests, Jan. 9, 1959, p. 4.

LATimes, FBI Captures Missing Duncan Case Figure, Jan. 19, 1959, p. 5.

LATimes, Kidnap-Killer Suspect Enters Insanity Plea, Feb. 11, 1959, p. 22.

LATimes, Gene Blake, Selection of Jury Starts in Duncan Murder Trial, Feb. 17, 1959, p. 2.

LATimes, Gene Blake, Duncan Trial Snagged by Death Penalty Wrangle, Feb. 19, 1959, p. 2.

LATimes, Gene Blake, Civil Liberties Union Enters Duncan Trial, Feb. 20, 1959, p. 2.

LATimes, Gene Blake, Eight Women, Four Men, Chosen on Duncan Jury, Feb. 21, 1959, p. 3.

LATimes, Mrs. Duncan Undergoes Brain Wave Studies, Feb. 24, 1959, p. D2.

LATimes, Judge to Rule Today on Mrs. Duncan's Sanity, March 24, 1959, p. 2.

LATimes, Gene Blake, Mrs. Duncan Tried to Hire Her to Kill, Carhop Says, Feb. 25, 1959, p. 2.

LATimes, Gene Blake, Mrs. Duncan's Threat to Kill Told in Court, Feb. 26, 1959, p. 2.

LATimes, Gene Blake, Mrs. Duncan's Threats to Daughter-In-Law Told, Feb. 28, 1959, p. B1.

LATimes, Gene Blake, Prosecution Rests Case in Duncan Murder Trial, Mar. 4, 1959, p. 2.

LATimes, Gene Blake, Mrs. Duncan Admits She Plotted to Kidnap Her Son, Mar. 5, 1959, p. 2.

LATimes, Gene Blake, Mrs. Duncan Wed 11 Times, Had 6 Children, DA Claims, Mar. 6, 1959, p. 2.

LATimes, Gene Blake, Duncan Takes Stand, Backs Mother's Story, Mar. 7, 1959, p. 3.

LATimes, Gene Blake, Hint of Death Threat Raised in Trial of Mrs. Duncan, Mar. 11, 1959, p. 2.

LATimes, Gene Blake, Attorneys End Arguments in Duncan Case, Mar. 12, 1959, p. B1.

LATimes, Gene Blake, Mrs. Duncan Guilty, Jury Told by District Attorney, Mar. 12, 1959, p.2.

LATimes, Gene Blake, Mrs. Duncan Lashes Back with Epithet at Prosecutor, Mar. 13, 1959, p. 2.

LATimes, Gene Blake, Find Mrs. Duncan Guilty of Murder, Mar. 17, 1959, p. 1.

LATimes, Gene Blake, Mrs. Duncan Shady Past, Vice Arrest Told at Trial, Mar. 18, 1959, p. 2.

LATimes, Gene Blake, Laughter Nearly Breaks Up Mrs. Duncan's Trial for Life, Mar. 19, 1959, p. 2.

LATimes, Gene Blake, Mrs. Duncan Isn't Insane, Psychiatrist Says at Trial, Mar. 20, 1959, p. 2.

LATimes, Gene Blake, Jury Says Death for Mrs. Duncan, Mar. 21, 1959, p. 1.

LATimes, Judge to Rule Today on Mrs. Duncan's Sanity, March 24, 1959, p. 2.

LATimes, Gene Blake, Mrs. Duncan Held Sane, Faces Death, Mar. 25, 1959, p. 1.

LATimes, Gene Blake, Mrs. Duncan Gets Death Sentence, Apr. 3, 1959, p. 3.

LATimes, Death for Baldonado Decreed in Duncan Case, Apr. 10, 1959, p. 5.

LATimes, Trial of Moya, Accused in Duncan Case, Begins, Apr. 21, 1959, p. 15.

LATimes, Wally George, Strictly Off the Record, Jun. 20, 1959, p. B6.

LATimes, Times Men Capture Sweepstakes, 4 Other Awards in Photo Contest, Feb. 5, 1960, p. B1.

LATimes, Duncan Death Decree Upheld, Mar. 12, 1960, p. 2.

LATimes, Mrs. Duncan Denied Murder Case Rehearing, Apr. 7, 1960, p. 4.

LATimes, Duncan Slayers Stay Sought, Jun. 4, 1960, p. 10.

LATimes, Mrs. Duncan Loses Appeal to Stay Death, Jun. 9, 1960, p. 4.

LATimes, Mrs. Duncan Doomed by U.S. Supreme Court, May 23, 1961, p. 2.

LATimes, Final Efforts to Save Mrs. Duncan Started, Aug. 1, 1961, p. 26.

LATimes, U.S. Judge Denies Plea to Free Mrs. Duncan, Aug. 10, 1961, p. B2.

LATimes, Drivers and Bus Line Apologize for Tie Up, Aug. 11, 1961, p. 20.

LATimes, Mrs. Duncan's Son, Partner Secretly Wed, Aug. 18, 1961, p. A12.

LATimes, Industrial Survey Sees Sales Boost, Aug. 22, 1961, p. 19.

LATimes, Mrs. Duncan's Pleas Submitted, Jan. 13, 1962, p. 15.

LATimes, Mrs. Duncan Appeals Again to High Court, Mar. 30, 1962, p. B19.

LATimes, High Court to Review Sit-in Trespass Cases, Jun. 26, 1962, p. 10.

LATimes, The State, Aug. 5, 1962, p. K5.

LATimes, Duncan After Mother's Death, Aug. 9, 1962, p. 3.

LATimes, Funeral Held For Duncan Case Figure, Aug. 9, 1962, p. 16.

LATimes, Howard Hertel, Mrs. Duncan Dies with 2 Coconspirators, Aug. 9, 1962, p. 1.

LATimes, Mrs. Duncan's Son Divorced, Jun. 20, 1966, p. A3.

7 MRS. GLADYS BAKER ELEY

Mrs. Gladys Baker Eley "had a mental breakdown shortly after the birth of her daughter, Norma Jean Baker, who later became the world-famous Marilyn Monroe," according to the LATimes. She spent most of her life in mental hospitals thereafter.

In July 1963, Gladys was found outside of Lakeview Terrace Baptist Church at 11901 Foothill Blvd., in the San Fernando Valley, after escaping from Rockhaven Sanitarium, 2713 Honolulu Ave., in Glendale, CA, by "lowering herself from a closet window," which was 8 feet off the ground. She tied two uniforms together to make a rope to escape with and had to squeeze through an 18 inch square window to enter the closet she escaped from. She also climbed over a wire mesh fence to leave the grounds. She walked the 15 miles between the sanitarium and the church. She was 60 years old at the time, and spent the night squeezed in the water heater closet outside the church. She was found waiting on the church steps and was met by Reverend J. Brian Reid, to whom she said that god told her to sleep in the water heater closet as it would be warm. Rev. Reid said she had a bible and a Science Christian book in her hands and was dressed in a white uniform. She told the reverend that she wanted to leave the sanitarium because they would not let her practice her religion. She was returned to Rockhaven Sanitarium.

In June 22, 1965, the Times published an article with the headline, "Marilyn Monroe Debts, Taxes Erase $1 Million: Nothing Left for Actress' Beneficiaries Or To Pay Bills of Her Mentally Ill Mother." The article said that there was approximately $4,000 owed to Rockhaven Sanitarium. In 1965, Marilyn's mother was 63 years old and had been in Rockhaven for the past 12 years. Marilyn had bequeathed $100,000 in a trust fund to pay $5,000 a year for her mother's care, but when she died, debts consumed Marilyn's funds and the money never was given to her mother after Marilyn's death. At some point, Gladys was transferred to Camarillo State Hospital for the LATimes reported in 1966, at age 64, she moved to Gainsville, Florida to live with her daughter Mrs. Bernice Miracle. Ms. Miracle reportedly arranged her release from Camarillo State Hospital and sent her money for the plane ticket to move to Florida.

LATimes, Metropolitan, Nov. 20, 1966, p. A.

LATimes, Art Berman, Marilyn Monroe Debts, Taxes Erase $1 Million, Jun. 22, 1965, p. 3.

LATimes, Marilyn Monroe Mother Flees Sanitarium, Found, Jul. 6, 1963, p. 14.

8 43 YEAR OLD SCHIZOID-PARANOID PATIENT

In June, 1972, Mrs. Frieda Franklin, age 47, was on trial for stealing $4,600 from a 43 year old schizoid-paranoid female patient who was transferred to her care from Camarillo State Hospital. Mrs. Franklin ran a board and care home at 11608 Kagel Canyon Street in Lakeview Terrace, and the home was licensed by the state Department of Social Welfare. The patient had $4,600 in a Sherman Oaks bank, and Mrs. Franklin got the patient to sign checks for "expenses" and finally transferred all of the money to a Van Nuys bank where the defendant withdrew it. The patient was found competent to testify as a witness in the case, and Mrs. Franklin was found guilty of grand theft. The patient was assigned to Mrs. Franklin's home by the County Department of Public Social Services and this department said it would ask the state to revoke Mrs. Franklin's license due to the conviction.

LATimes, Care Home Operator Will Be Sentenced, Jun. 23, 1972, p. SF2.

9 MRS. MARJORIE HAAS

On July 25, 1953, just after midnight, a home at 5010 Fountain Ave. in West Hollywood burst into a gas fire. Mrs. Marjorie Ann Haas, age 22, was taken to the General Hospital by an ambulance and she was said to have first, second and third degree burns on her body. The fire battalion chief said that Marjorie lit a match in a bedroom of the home "after a gas stove had been leaking in the bathroom for some time." The explosion cost several thousand dollars in damages. On Nov. 14, 1956, less than three years later, the Times reported that Mrs. Marjorie Haas had accidentally smothered her 2 1/2 year old baby, Virginia, to death at 5010 Fountain Ave. It took police an hour to convince the mother the baby was dead, as the mother continued to cling to the body of the child. Marjorie was 25 years old and "on probation" from Camarillo Mental Hospital when this happened. She lived in her home with her mother and grandmother and said she thought the baby's father was in Florida.

LATimes, Gas Explosion Burns Woman, Jul. 25, 1953, p. 1.

LATimes, Mother Clings to Baby Smothered in Crib, Nov. 15, 1956, p. B6.

10 DELIGA HARP

Deliga, 38, and her husband Ruel F. Harp, 36 were found guilty of child neglect on Jan. 10, 1946. They were sentenced to 180 days in the County Jail. Police said the couple had been arrested numerous times for intoxication and peace disturbance. Their four children, Beverly Joan, 12; Barbara, 9; Rose Marie, 7; and Ruel Francis, jr., 2, were placed in protective custody with the state. Judge Lester O. Luce recommended Mrs. Harp be committed to Camarillo State Hospital and Mr. Harp be sent to the Castaic Honor Farm.

LATimes, Couple Given Jail Sentence, Jan. 11, 1946, p. A3.

11 MRS. DORA HERRERA

In late Feb. 1973, Dr. Robert Manniello, age 27, was examining patient charts in a hospital emergency room. Dora Herrera then burst in with an ice pick and stabbed it "almost to the hilt" into the doctor's back, between his shoulder blades. Two women on staff at the time chased Dora, who left the hospital into the streets. The two women aides said they could not get help from anyone on the street while they looked for Mrs. Herrera. She was found in a local store and police were called. When police arrived, Mrs. Herrera was standing in line to buy ice cream. The hospital said that Mrs. Herrera had brought a 6 month old baby to the hospital a week prior and was dissatisfied with treatment received. It was believed she was babysitting the child. It was determined that Mrs. Herrera was a former patient at Camarillo State Hospital and she was charged with assault with the intent to commit murder.

LATimes, Woman Seized in Store, Feb. 27, 1973, p. 3.

12 TARA ANN KATONA

Tara Ann Katona was diagnosed with manic depression in 1978, at age 17, and began taking lithium at that time to control the highs and lows. She stopped taking her lithium in 1983, and her moods got worse. Her mother, Stena Katona, age 42, said Tara would slam her body into walls, almost involuntarily, and thought people were "against her." She was committed to Camarillo State Hospital in April 1983 by County mental health workers because she threw herself at a truck in the street. Tara spent April – August of 1983 in three different mental institutions, moving in and out as she oscillated between depression and calm. In August 1983, Tara went to her boyfriend's house, held his gun to her head, and pulled the trigger but there was no bullet inside. She was returned to Camarillo at this point for suicidal tendencies.

In September 1983, Tara was being treated at Camarillo for severe mental depression. Her mother told her "to look beyond the room she was in, to look outside at the palm trees," and she said her daughter replied, "I can't see the beauty anymore." Tara had spent a year skiing in Colorado and was an aspiring actress who lived in Reseda and worked in convalescent homes and restaurants. She took classes at Pierce College. Tara's mother said she felt her daughter was still suicidal upon release from Camarillo State Hospital.

The day before her daughter's release from Camarillo, on Sept. 13, 1983, Tara's mom was told by the hospital counselor that she had put a down payment on a Colt .38-caliber Special (gun) a month prior when she was out, in August. Tara's boyfriend told the mother she was trying to buy the gun from National Gun Sales, Inc. in Northridge, and so the mother called the gun store and told them not to sell the gun to her daughter because she was suicidal and just being released from a mental hospital. The mother claims the gun store said they would not sell the gun to her suicidal daughter and said she felt relieved.

On Sept. 14, at age 22, Tara checked out of Camarillo saying if she did not check out then, she might never gain the courage to leave there again. On Sept. 16, 1983, Tara did not show up for a counseling appointment and her mother became alarmed. She called the gun store to make sure they did not sell her the gun, and this time, she says the gun store said they could not tell her that as it was an invasion of privacy. The mother assumed that meant they sold her the gun and started trying to reach her daughter by phone. After work, the mother went to her home and was going to go to Tara's apartment but upon arriving at her own home, she was told her daughter had killed herself in the apt. she shared with others, and one of her roommates found her dead. The mother joined a group called Compassionate Friends of the Valley, which is a group for bereaved parents and said she is thankful for her other 4 children, who helped her get through the loss of Tara a little easier.

Tara's mother and father sued the gun store for $2 million for selling the gun to Tara when they knew she was suicidal and had been contacted by her mother the day before. Gloria Allred was the attorney for the parents in this case. Allred accused the gun store of violating a state "Welfare and Institutions Code section banning sale of any "deadly weapon" to a mental patient in a hospital or on leave of absence from the hospital," according to the Times. The Times also said the court had to decide whether Tara Ana was fully released or on a leave from Camarillo Hospital to decide if that would apply in her case. The law suit also claimed there was a breach of contract due to the promise not to sell the gun to Tara Ann and also accused the gun shop of interfering with her efforts to "rescue" her daughter from a suicide.

In March 1986, the Northridge gun shop that sold Tara Ann the gun settled out of court with her parents for $175,000. They acknowledge no liability with the settlement. Later, in April 1986, another family sued a Van Nuys gun shop for selling their mentally ill son a gun which he used in his suicide, using the Katona case as precedence.

LATimes, Jan Klunder, Daughter Killed Herself, "Couldn't See Beauty Anymore," Dec. 25, 1983, p. V1.

LATimes Myrna Oliver, $2 Million Sought From Gun Shop in Suicide, Nov. 29, 1983, p. C1.

LATimes, Elizabeth Lu, Gun Seller, Hospital Sued in Suicide, Apr. 1, 1986, p. V_A7.

LA Times, The Region, Mar. 14, 1986, p. SD2.

Caged windows in South Quad (Photo: K. Anderberg 2010)

13 MIRIAM KIM

Miriam Kim was a former clerk at the Olive View Sanatorium, and was placed under a citizen's arrest by her boss Glenn Henry Hymer, an administrative assistant at Olive View, on Nov. 29, 1955. Hymer said Kim had "attempted several times to kiss him." When she did not show up for the hearing, charges were dropped as it was revealed that Miss Kim had been committed to Camarillo State Hospital "on a complaint signed by a family member."

LATimes, Kiss Case Dismissed, Dec. 20, 1955, p. 24.

14 MRS. MYRTLE NELL KLINKER

Myrtle Nell Klinker was committed to Camarillo Hospital in 1941 for mental incompetence. Her husband, Lawrence E. Klinger divorced Myrtle in Las Vegas on March 16, 1945, and then married his new wife the following day. In March 1950, Mrs. Klinger sued the trust company in charge of her estate saying the divorce was not valid and her own property had been transferred in the marriage. The courts found in favor of the husband and his second wife. The second wife claimed the stress from the lawsuits made her ill and caused her public humility and asked for $33,000 in restitution for malicious prosecution.

LATimes, Woman Seeks Damages for Estate Suit, Mar. 9, 1950, p. A2.

Abandoned patient room with exam lights at bed level in South Quad (Photo: K. Anderberg, Feb. 19, 2011).

Courtyard in South Quad with typical tile fountains present in so many of the courtyards…to the right is the forensic courtroom and the rest of the ward is isolation rooms, nurses' stations and offices. (Photo: K. Anderberg, Feb. 19, 2011)

Beautiful wrought iron grates guard stairwells to prevent patients from jumping. This grate is in the South Quad. (Photo: K. Anderberg, 2010).

Abandoned Camarillo State Hospital, South Quad (Photo: K. Anderberg, 2009)

Another stairwell grate in the South Quad (Photo: K. Anderberg, 2010)

View from inside an abandoned day room in the receiving and treatment building which is now the library building at CSUCI. You can see how the courtyard is surrounded on all sides by the building and the doors have several layers of bars on them. (K. Anderberg, 2010)

Shadow at midday on wall of South Quad isolation room (Photo: K. Anderberg, 2010)

South Quad, Units 28/29 (Photo: K. Anderberg, 2010)

Nurses' station in receiving and treatment building (Photo: K. Anderberg, 2011)

Collection of floor tiles from the old hospital I found in dump heaps behind the old hospital. Most of these tiles were made in the 1930's. Colors for the hexagon tiles range from brown to several shades of green, yellow, black, white and gray. Other tiles I have found are pink and cobalt blue. (Photo: K. Anderberg, 2011)

Camarillo State Hospital Plaque on front of South Quad Bell Tower, lists dedication of the plaque as Oct. 12, 1936. (Photo: K. Anderberg, 2011)

Isolation rooms very close together and only big enough for one bed, with curtains still hanging, in Unit 28/29 in the South Quad. (Photo: K.Anderberg 2011)

Dining hall in North Quad (Photo: K. Anderberg, 2011)

The old bandstand in the middle of the North Quad is now gone. It has been removed in the remodeling of the grounds for CA State University at Channel Islands' campus. The banstand was a favorite of patients, and local bands would provide free concerts for the patients outside in this area. (Photo: K. Anderberg 2010)

Children's Mural outside the receiving and treatment building, inside fenced yard (Photo: K. Anderberg 2010)

15 JOAN KRIEG

Miriam Kim Joan Krieg was a 24 year old North Hollywood housewife when she was arrested for the suspected murder of her 3 children in October 1966. Joan was accused of drowning her 2 sons, James Thomas Krieg, jr., age 4, and Robert, who was 9 months old, and stabbing her 3 year old daughter Debra. She supposedly left the dead children in the upstairs bathroom and then went downstairs to wait for her husband to come home from work. James Krieg, 32, returned home from his job as an aircraft mechanic to find the children dead. The Times report she was taken to the Valley Doctors' Hospital due to a "self-inflicted superficial stab wound" and was also given an antidote for something she drank as an attempted suicide. Afterwards, she was charged with murder and held at the General Hospital's prison ward. Mr. Krieg told police that his wife had been in both Camarillo State Mental Hospital and Los Angeles County General Hospital for mental difficulties.

On Jan. 2, 1966, 10 months before she was accused of murdering her children, Joan Krieg was pictured in the L.A.Times, holding her new baby, with the caption, "Mrs. Joan Krieg with son, Robert, who shared honor of being the first borne in 1966." The article is about the first babies borne in the L.A. area in the New Year, and says Robert was born one second after midnight at the Hollywood Presbyterian Hospital.

LATimes, Housewife, 24, Held in Death of 3 Children, Oct. 9, 1966, p. G6.

LATimes, Two Arrive Split Second in New Year, Jan. 2, 1966, p. B3.

16 RONNIE RAE

Ronnie Rae, a 23 year old singer, went to an audition for Steve Cochran, an actor, at his home and later tried to sue him for beating her in his home at 3401 Coldwater Canyon Lane, on Dec. 2, 1964. An investigation showed Ronnie had gone "berserk" after the audition and there was another man and woman present, at the time. Witnesses said that Ronnie tried to jump into a stone fireplace, threw herself into walls and onto the floor, screamed profanities, and said she was going to jump off the cliff outside the home.

On Dec. 5, 1964, the Times reported that Ronnie had told police that she had been invited to Cochran's home to play some recordings of songs she had written for him, but then she says she spilled a drink, and Cochran then bound her hands and feet with neckties, beat her and gagged her with a towel. Cochran showed up at the police station saying instead that she had gone downstairs, and when he found her, she was throwing herself into walls, diving into the fireplace and saying "Steve Cochran is trying to kill me!" He was willing to take a lie detector test to prove he was telling the truth. He also said he was suing Ronnie for slander and malicious prosecution.

Cochran said his assistant, Mark Miller, was the one that tied her up but that Cochran helped his assistant lift her up. Cochran said he had never seen the woman before that day and also noted he was never alone with her the entire time. Cochran said that Ronnie had come recommended by a woman working on one of his films and that was how the meeting occurred. He said she seemed normal when she arrived.

Cochran did not show up for questioning by police for two days after said crime supposedly took place. He said he had been out on a boat and did not know police were looking for him. Ronnie said that her 72 year old grandmother "rescued" her from Cochran's house. Police said there were conflicts in the testimony so they would interview more witnesses before deciding whether to file criminal charges in the case.

On Dec. 8, 1964, the District Attorney announced it would not press criminal charges against Steve Cochran when it was discovered that Ronnie had attempted suicide numerous times in the past. The Deputy District Attorney on the case, Paul Esnard, said they "probably did a great service in tying her up." It was noted that Ronnie was released from Camarillo State Hospital in September 1964, with recommendations that she receive further treatment.

On Jan. 22, 1965, Ronnie Rae pled guilty to disturbing the peace due, to an incident that led to her arrest on Nov. 22. Ronnie was arrested at approximately 7 AM for sleeping in a car on Wilshire Blvd. It was noted the incident with Steve Cochran occurred less than two weeks later, on Dec. 3, 1965. The judge dismissed a $25 fine, and withdrew two other charges related to her having possession of hypnotic drugs at the time of the arrest. It was discovered that the drugs were tranquilizers which were prescribed by her doctor legally.

LATimes, Steve Cochran Denies Tying, Beating Singer, Dec. 5, 1964, p. 15.

LATimes, Singer Denied Action Against Steve Cochran, Dec. 9, 1964, p. 3.

LATimes, Ronnie Rae Drug Charge Dismissed, Jan. 23, 1965, p. B2.

17 MRS. FRANCES C. ROBINSON

Mrs. Frances C. Robinson was married to the son of Edward G. Robinson, the actor, and had a child, Francesca Robinson, with Edward G. Robinson, jr. On March 23, 1964, Frances, aged 33, was committed to Camarillo State Hospital by a judge in psychopathic court. In a custody hearing in late March 1964, Mrs. Gladys Lloyd Robinson, aged 67, the maternal grandmother of Francesca who was 11 years old at the time, and Mrs. Augustine Whitehead, aged 67, who was once the governess for Edward G. Robinson, jr., (who was then 31 years old), petitioned for custody of the young girl. Although Frances was incarcerated at Camarillo Hospital, the attorney for Frances asked she be allowed to weigh in with her feelings about the change of custody and thus the hearing postponed until the following month. Frances had custody of Francesca since her 1955 divorce from Edward Robinson, jr.

LATimes, Court Holds Up Decision on Star's Kin, Mar. 26, 1964, p. 24.

18 GIOVANNA SCOGLIO AKA GIA SCALA

Mrs. Frances C. Gia Scala, whose real name is Giovanna Scoglio, was described as a tall green eyed actress who was born in Europe. She was in the 1955 movie, "All That Heaven Allows," as well as other movies, including "Never Say Goodbye," "Big Boodle," "Battle of the Coral Sea," "Don't Go Near the Water" with Glenn Ford, and "The Guns of Navarone" with Gregory Peck. Many articles in the LATimes from the 1950's hail Scala as a popular actress, and follow her adventures with the Hollywood elite.

In 1955, Scala signed a contract with Universal Pictures, and her first film was "All That Heaven Allows."

In Nov. 1956, the Times wrote, "make a note to watch the screen appearance of a young woman named Gia Scala, one of the most arresting personalities to reach Hollywood in a long while." This article also said her "charm and beauty were finally recognized both by Universal and Columbia, which now share her contract."

On Jan. 24, 1957, Scala had met the five years' residency in the U.S. to apply for citizenship, and went to the U.S. Dept. of Immigration and Naturalization to apply for U.S. citizenship. She was borne in England but grew up primarily in Rome.

On August 1, 1957, the Times reported Scala was arrested in West Los Angeles for misdemeanor drunk driving when her car missed a curve and drove into a building off of Highway 101 at Chatauqua Blvd. She said she had drunk 2 glasses of champagne prior to driving, and said she was not drunk when police insisted she was and arrested her. She paid her own bail with $392 she had in her purse when arrested, then complained this would probably ruin her as people would think she was drunk, which she still denied. She said that she may have to return to Rome due to this charge. The actress who was in sandals and a sleeveless sweater when arrested, later said she had been on her way to the beach that night when she got into the accident. She said she had the champagne with the doctor who was treating her ailing mother and that she wanted to go look at the ocean for a while, which she liked to do. She said she could face the criticism of this from Hollywood, but dreaded her mother finding out.

On Aug. 2, 1957, drunk driving charges were dropped against Gia in a West Los Angeles court for lack of evidence. Gia was wearing a bandage on her right leg supposedly from an injury from the car crash, and showed up in court with two "Universal International" attorneys, aka studio hired guns, to protect their client, to plead her case.

In Dec. 1957, Scala was in a film that teamed her up with Glenn Ford, called "Don't Go Near the Water."

On April 30, 1958, Scala became a U.S. citizen.

On Aug. 5, 1958, Scala was grabbed off a stone parapet as she "teetered" over the River Thames on the Waterloo Bridge. A cab driver grabbed Scala while calling for police on his radio. The cab driver said Scala had called him to pick her up at her apt. at midnight, and asked to be driven to the Waterloo Bridge for a "rendezvous." Police took her to the police station where at first she would not give her name and she slept the night at the police station, reportedly in "partial shock." Scala's father retrieved her from the police station on Aug. 6, and took her home.

Less than a month after she was pulled from a bridge, on Aug. 28, 1958, the Times showed a picture of a young, vibrant Scala smoking a cigar with a big smile on her face, with the caption, "Screen actress Gia Scala adds a new twist to her pose by holding a cigar for photographers during luncheon with a party of friends at London hotel. Having dared that much, she later smoked stogie."

On Aug. 21, 1959, Gia married Donald J. Burnett, who was described as a TV actor. He was said to be working for Metro studios on a TV show called Northwest Passage. She said they met at the Metro studio lots as they both worked there. She commented on liking a husband that was an actor as he could understand her world. They were married at City Hall and it was the first marriage for both of them.

In Sept. 1959, Scala was interviewed by Lydia Lane for the Beauty section of the Times. She said, "I am dieting again, I wish the Americans did not like their women so slim, the Latins don't. I made a picture in Cuba and the men there prefer curves, but here they would call you fat." She said the first thing the studios said to her was she needed to lose 10 pounds, so she did, but she said she gained it back. She said ever since she came to Hollywood she had been dieting, and it was reported she was eating tomatoes and eggs as the reporter and her spoke. She said dieting has been a "constant struggle" and commented she was reading about health and was going to learn to like foods without fat. She also said she is making sure to exercise, saying she likes a walk after dinner and that she had just signed up for ballet classes. The reporter commented she liked Scala's "scent," and the two discussed perfume. Scala said she loves perfume and has learned to buy it in little bottles because it evaporates so fast. The reporter asked if she was "fickle with perfumes" and Scala said she only used one fragrance at a time, something light in the morning and something exotic and romantic for the evening. She said her mother used to go out and gather dew to put on her face in the morning, and that she did that too to help keep her healthy complexion.

In Sept. 1963, the Times ran another article with Scala about dieting, again with Lydia Lane. She said before she was married and before she was contracted to Columbia, she had trouble with her weight. She said, "I thought the less I ate, the more I would lose, but it doesn't work that way." She said the harder she tried to lose, the more miserable she got and said she wanted to talk to other girls so they did not make her mistakes. She said she was eating the wrong foods, and a snack cart would come by and she would be starving, so she would eat foods that were not good for her. She said she resented being criticized and nagged at about her weight and said sometimes she ate just out of "defiance." She said once she was married and making three meals a day for her husband, she began to eat more but of better foods and lost weight without effort. The Times offered a "Vitality Diet" for "more energy and reducing without fatigue," written by Scala, which consisted of 3 well-planned meals a day, for 10 cents and a self-addressed stamped envelope.

Scala and her husband separated on Feb. 21, 1969. On Mar. 26, 1969, "stockbroker" Donald J. Burnett, age 38, agreed to pay Scala, age 35, $800 a month alimony and allowed her sole use of their Universal City home until their divorce trial was heard.

On April 20, 1971, Scala was arrested with Allen Bershin, a 22 year old busboy, in the parking lot of a restaurant on Figueroa St. for beating the parking lot attendant up over a fifty cent parking fee. Police said when they arrived all three were on the ground and the attendant said Scala and the busboy beat him up. Bershin was charged with assault and pled no contest, paid a $125 fine and was given 3 years' probation. Scala was charged with disturbing the peace and pled innocent. On April 22, 1971, Scala was sent to jail for this assault, since she could not raise a $500 bond to get out of jail. Her sister was at the hearing but did not have the money to bail her out. In court, the parking lot attendant said they did not pay to park, so he had blocked their car in and that is why they started to assault him. A picture in the LATimes dated May 12, 1971, shows Scala looking more like a disheveled criminal than a starlet as in the past. The busboy she is seen with looks very shady, as well. It is a far cry from the squeaky clean marriage photo run in the Times over 10 years prior. Scala's hearing was set for June 1, 1971.

On May 19, Scala was arrested for drunk driving and then later lost consciousness in the courtroom. At that point, the judge ordered her to Camarillo State Hospital for observation and examinations.

On June 1, 1971, Scala was supposed to show for a court date about the peace disturbance charge but when she did not show, it was revealed she was sent to Camarillo State Hospital for observation by a Ventura judge in the previous weeks.

On July 26, 1971, Scala was given 2 years' probation and fined $125 for the peace disturbance charge with the parking lot attendant. Judge Irwin Nebron congratulated her on looking like "another human being now," saying she looked in shambles two months prior in his courtroom when she first was charged with the crime. One of the conditions for her probation was she was not allowed to have contact with "known narcotics users." She became indignant and said she had never hung around those types of people, to which the judge replied he was merely giving standard directives. When asked in court by a jurist why her right index finger was in a splint, she said had severed her finger in a car crash 3 weeks prior and that the finger had been sewn back on by doctors.

On April 30, 1972, Scala, aged 36, was found dead in her Hollywood Hills home. The cause of death was thought to be an accidental drug overdose pending the autopsy. The autopsy revealed that Scala had severe coronary arteriosclerosis which was said to have contributed to her death, but her death was listed as an overdose of alcohol and drugs. She was buried in the Holy Cross Cemetery.

LATimes, John L. Scott, Fan Note Keep Eye on Starlett Gia Scala, Nov. 18, 1956, p. E3.

COMMITMENT CRITERIA

LATimes, Gia Scala of Films Seeking Citizenship, Jan. 25, 1957, p. B1.

LATimes, Edwin Schallert, "Twilight for Gods" Big Picture Purchase: Gia Scala to Lure Taylor, Feb. 4, 1957, p. C9.

LATimes, Actress Gia Scala Named as Drunk Driver, Aug. 2, 1957, p. B1.

LATimes, Gia Scala's Drunk Driving Case Dropped, Aug. 3, 1957, p. B1.

LATimes, Italian-Borne Actress Teams with Glenn Ford, Dec. 23, 1957, p. 17.

LATimes, Film Actress Gia Scala Becomes U.S. Citizen, Mar. 1, 1958, p. B1.

LATimes, Actress Gia Scala Pulled From Bridge, Aug. 6, 1958, p. 2.

LATimes, Photo Standalone 3 – No Title, Aug. 28, 1958, p. 3.

LATimes, Photo Standalone – No Title, Aug. 19. 1959, p. 5.

LATimes, Lydia Lane, Beauty, Sept. 20, 1959, D13.

LATimes, Hedda Hopper, Gia Scala, A Tempest in Any Language, Sept. 3 1961, A4.

LATimes, Lydia Lane, Beauty, Jan. 13, 1963, p. D10.

LATimes, Southland, Mar. 26, 1969, p. B2.

LATimes, Film Actress Jailed After Fight at Café, Apr 21, 1971, p. C2.

LATimes, Southland, Apr 22, 1971, p. 32A.

LATimes, Photo Standalone – No Title, May 12, 1971, p. 3.

LATimes, Judge Commits Gia for Observation, Jun. 2, 1971, p. B5.

LATimes, Gia Scala Sentenced in Disturbance, Jul. 27, 1971, p. B3.

LATimes, Actress Gia Scala, 36, Found Dead in Hollywood Hills Home, May 1, 1972, p. 3.

LATimes, Commuters Playing Actress Gia Scala Found Dead Part in Smog Test at Home Overdose Suspected, May 1, 1972, p. A3.

LATimes, Gia Scala Had Heart Condition, Autopsy Reveals, May 2, 1972, p. D1.

19 CATHERINE SMITH

Mrs. France Catherine Smith was a silent movie actress, and was found drowning in an oil pit in April 1942 at the age of 38. She died shortly after she was dragged out of the oil by rescuers. Barking dogs led rescuers to her and originally her cause of death was listed as a suicide, but when investigators went to her brother's house in Santa Fe Springs to question him about Catherine's death, they found his house burned down. Raymond F. Smith, age 50, was then charged by the Superior Court with arson. Smith said he burned down his house because he was tired of it, and said he should be able to burn down his house if he wants to since he owns it and had no plans to collect insurance or profit from it. Raymond became a suspect because on Jan. 5, 1942, he signed an insanity complaint against his sister, then a week later she was sent to Camarillo State Mental Hospital. She was "paroled" into his custody on March 1, 1942, and in April 1942, while living with Raymond, she was found drowning in an oil pit, which killed her.

On April 24, 1942, Raymond told police that Catherine had just thrown herself in the oil pool "during one of her spells." He denied having anything to do with it. When police asked Raymond about his signing her commitment papers to Camarillo Hospital, he said he signed "a paper" and said he did not know what it was. An ex-lover of Catherine's was sought for questioning about her relationship with her brother.

LATimes, Arson Suspect Held for Trial, Apr. 28, 1942, p. A8

LATimes, Mail Carrier Sticks to Story, Apr. 24, 1942, p. A12.

LATimes, Mailman Persists in Denial of His Sister's Death, Apr. 25. 1942, p. 6.

The Bowling Alley in the South Quad, now the Art Building of CSUCI (Photo: K. Anderberg, 2011)

20 PAULA STANWAY THORPE

Paula Thorpe, age 31, a nightclub singer, dancer and showgirl, who was known by her maiden/stage name Paula Stanway when she worked in Chicago and New York, married Carlyle Thorpe, age 58, by then a millionaire, on March 21, 1940. Both had come from pioneer families in the region. Paula was young, blonde, and quite attractive. Carlyle Thorpe, a man looking more like her father than her husband, was the head of a walnut growers' organization. They met at a Chicago nightclub where Paula was a dancer. Apparently they had gotten married in Berlin in August, 1939, when she was on tour as a dancer, and she said they stayed in the biggest hotel in Berlin after the wedding and "did up the town."

The couple wed again in Nevada in 1940 to make sure the marriage was legal. Throughout the early 1940's, there were many articles about Paula Thorpe's race horse stable and her winning horses. But by 1943, three years after their marriage, the articles in the papers were all about her divorce. Paula said on June 28, 1943, her husband expelled her from their mansion. The Times reports that in June 1943, Paula's husband hired a private detective to pose as an agent for a national magazine and that this person lured Paula into compromising positions at parties and in pictures, which she contends was her husband's goal. She also testified that her husband often brought "certain immoral women" into their house to entertain his business partners from out of town. Paula says her husband cursed at her and hit her in front of several friends and then said he would give her a few thousand dollars if she divorced him, but said he would give her nothing if she did not divorce him.
Paula said her community property ownings were $100,000 and included the couple's cash, securities and Stanway Stables, which had 28 race horses and mares, and was named after her maiden name, Stanway. She testified her

husband also made over $50,000 a year and owned over 1 million dollars in assets. Paula asked for $1000 a month in alimony to live separately from the man she had married who was nearly twice her age. In addition to the alimony, Paula asked the courts to force her husband to pay her $2500 in court fees and $15,000 in attorney fees.

On July 30, 1943, Paula collapsed in the hall outside the courtroom for her alimony hearing. She was taken to the medics at City Hall, was said to quickly recompose herself and went back to the courtroom. Judge William S. Baird presided and awarded Paula $400 a month, rather than the $1000 a month she had asked for, and also awarded her attorney fee payments of $5000, not the $15000 she had requested. Paula continued to charge that her husband brought prostitutes to their house which sometimes spent the night. Carlyle immediately filed cross-suits against his ex-wife charging her with misconduct and having 3 "John Does" named as co-respondents.

Joseph Lorne Hoover, age 30, was one of these John Does. He testified in a deposition dated Sept. 1941, according to the LATimes, that he visited the Thorpe's mansion with a man who was dating one Carlyle's daughters by a different marriage. Hoover testified that Carlyle was not present on the night he visited the mansion and that at 4 AM, he followed Paula up to her bedroom. Hoover says he spent several hours there, sitting in a chair and reclining on the bottom of her bed but he says he did not have any intimacy with Paula. Hoover admits he was drunk that evening, after drinking with Paula and her stepdaughter and his friend, and said he may not remember all that was done and said.

Another one of the John Does was John L. Scroggs, a former film actor, who later worked in the Navy. He testified that between Christmas 1942 and New Year's Day 1943, Paula came to his hotel downtown and "they had indulged in some drinking." Joe Snider was another man to testify against Paula in her alimony hearing. He was hired by the stable trainer, Ray Slomer, and testified that Ray and Paula had "romantic interludes" which included holding hands in public, kissing, and calling each other pet names. Snider testified that sometimes when he would enter the area of these romantic interludes, they would stop in his presence. The Times said this was the third time Paula had been accused of "indescretions" with other men, citing Hoover and Scroggs as the first two, even though Scroggs merely said she drank with him and Hoover swears nothing intimate happened.
On Nov. 26, 1943, a fourth male was brought to the courts to testify on behalf of Carlyle Thorpe against his wife Paula in their divorce and alimony law suit. James S. Somers said in his deposition that he went to the Thorpe mansion in Sept. 1941 while Carlyle was not home, and said he noticed

something "odd" about Paula while he was dancing with her. Somers was 16 years old at the time. He said she was holding him close and giving him "little kisses" on his neck. Later, he said she took him to the garage where they sat in her car as she put her arms around the young Somers and kissed him. He said he left the party at around 1 AM but that his friends Hoover and another man, Ronald Van Pohlmann, were still at the party when he left.

Ronald Van Pohlmann was the 5th man to testify against Paula on behalf of her husband Carlyle. He said during that during this alleged party in Sept. 1941, he witnessed Hoover and Paula in her bedroom "in their nightclothes."

On Jan. 22, 1944, Ray Slomer filed a deposition denying he ever kissed or was intimate with Paula, as was said in a deposition from Joe Snider, an ex-assistant to Slomer at the Stanway Stables. He said he thought of Paula more as a sister, not a lover. Joe Snider also said he had quit working for Slomer because he frequently asked Snider to freeze the horses' feet before races. Slomer denies having asked Snider to freeze the horses' feet frequently and said he only asked him to do that one time because the horse had a bowed tendon.

On Jan. 25, 1944, Superior Judge Myron Westover named a neutral doctor to assess Paula's health as the two parties' doctors' testimonies were conflicting. Apparently Paula had submitted reports from a Santa Barbara doctor saying she was too ill to go through the hearing process at that point, and her attorney asked for a 10 week delay in the hearing for her recovery. Carlyle's attorney countered with a report by a different Santa Barbara doctor who said he had examined Paula a week prior in the hospital and that, though she was nervous due to the hearing, that nervousness would leave once the hearing was over, thus she was not too ill to attend the hearing. The request to delay the hearing 10 weeks was denied, but due to a new doctor being assigned to determine Paula's state of health, the hearing was postponed until the end of February.

On March 24, 1944, the 4th day of the divorce hearings, Daphne Thorpe Lindstrom, Paula's 19 year old stepdaughter who had attended the infamous "chop suey party" on Sept. 13, 1941, took the stand. Daphne said Paula had been wearing a "filmy negligee" and a "white satin nightgown" on her bed in the master bedroom that night and that Hoover and Von Pohlmann were guests that evening. Daphne said Hoover was wearing her father's "dressing gown" with bare feet and was spread across the base of the bed, with his feet handing over the end of the bed. She said that her and Von Pohlmann went into the bedroom and sat down and talked to Paula and Hoover for a while. She said she left back to her room with Von Pohlmann but returned to

Paula's room again and spoke to them, and Hoover was in the exact same position he had originally been in. She returned to her room and Von Pohlmann went to the guest room. When Daphne returned to the master bedroom once again, the door was locked so she did not knock. Daphne testified they had been drinking Bourbon from the bar at the house and said Paula told her if she said anything negative about her to her father, she would send Daphne to boarding school, which Daphne said scared her as she looked at boarding school as a sort of prison.

On March 28, 1944, Carlyle testified that a prenuptial agreement said that he had to put $125 a month plus another $300 a month for spending money into an account for Paula every month they were married so that if they broke up, she would not be destitute. Carlyle testified that Paula said she would not ask for alimony from him, or any man, saying she saw such actions as gold-digging. He said the longer they stayed married, the more money would accrue for her to leave with due to the arrangement. Carlyle said the money he had put aside for Paula was then spent when she opened a stable for race horses and hired a trainer she was seen walking hand in hand with everywhere, as he said he sat around "like a bump on a log."

On March 29, 1944, a private detective named Ruthie Stanford took the stand on behalf of Carlyle. He had paid Ruthie to spy on Paula. Ruthie testified that in June 1943, Paula, her friend Betty Peyton and Betty's 18 or 19 year old son Lynn, and Ruthie, were on a trip in Tijuana, Mexico, when there was a shortage of hotel rooms, and so they all had to share a room. Ruthie testified that as she and Betty pretended to be asleep, Ruthie watched Paula, who was naked but for a white garter belt, as she "allowed" Lynn to light her cigarette. Ruthie said Betty told Paula to put some clothes on, and so she put on Betty's son's undershirt. Ruthie said she was hired by Carlyle to investigate his wife's drinking, and had posed as a reporter wanting to write a story about her and her horses.

Ruthie testified a few days after the Tijuana incident, she saw the young Lynn and Paula drink 14 double shots of Scotch at a café where they all met. Ruthie said she did not drink or smoke and ordered limeades while Paula and Lynn drank Scotch. She said the three of them then went to a nightclub together, where Paula and Lynn drank more and a photo taken of the three on that evening was entered into evidence. Ruthie commented that Paula said to watch out for spies following them, unaware Ruthie was a spy in the car with them. Paula was not in the courtroom during these testimonies as she was deemed too ill to attend the hearings.

On Mar. 30, 1944, Betty Peyton took the stand and said Ruthie Stanford, the detective, was a liar. She said her son, Lynn, who was at that point in the Navy overseas, had never touched a drop of hard liquor, had never drank liquor with Paula, nor had he ever had sex with Paula. Of the night they all spent in Tijuana, Betty testified that the three women shared a double bed and the young boy slept on a cot in the room. She testified under oath that her son undressed in the bathroom then went to sleep in the cot. She said at no time did he undress in front of Paula and at no time was Paula ever nude in front of her son.

In April 1944, Carlyle was granted a divorce from Paula.

On Aug. 11, 1944, Judge Stanley Mosk denied Paula alimony but awarded her $1000 in attorney fees and $1500 for upcoming attorney fees for an appeal.

On Feb. 15, 1945, Paula called Carlyle and asked for money, which he refused to give her. Carlyle said his offer still stood to give her $5000 if she dropped the appeal, but if not, he said he would give her nothing. Paula said she would take $30,000 to drop the appeal. A few hours later, she took poison at her apt., attempting suicide. Paula said the $5000 Carlyle offered would barely cover taxes, legal and hospital fees. Paula was taken to the General Hospital to recover from the suicide attempt. On Feb. 17, 1945, the Times reported that Paula's health was improving.

On March 22, 1945, Paula attempted to take the stand at her alimony hearing yet she was reportedly hysterical, collapsed, and was brought into the courtroom on a cot by ambulance medics. Her attorney explained she had attempted suicide the month prior, taking corrosive poison and sleeping pills, because she was tired of "trying to buck three or four million dollars." She said they wanted her doctor to tell them what was wrong with her but would not pay them. Her doctor gave her sedatives in the courtroom at this point. She said she wanted to get on the witness stand and said the courts were not allowing her to testify as court went into recess. Paula's doctor testified that she was very ill and required the care of a doctor and nurse if she was not to die. The doctor on cross-examination said that he did not do diagnostic tests that would have been reasonable because she was too sick to be "subjected to diagnostic procedure." Carlyle argued in court that his status as a millionaire was exaggerated to which Paula's attorney retorted that he could prove Carlyle was a millionaire if the court so requested.

On March 24, 1945, Judge Dudley S. Valentine denied Paula's petition for $1000 monthly alimony pending the appeal of the divorce a year prior.

On Oct. 22, 1945, Paula went to the Superior Court again with a petition for support, saying she was in dire need of medical attention and hospitalization. Her attorney said that money was necessary to save the life of the actress. Paula was carried into the courtroom on a stretcher, and her doctor said she was down to 78 pounds from her usual 120 pounds. Carlyle testified at this hearing that Paula had threatened his life in August 1945. He said she called him and said she was armed with a weapon and asked him to meet her. He also said she left a note in his mailbox that said "I'll catch up with you yet."

On Dec. 14, 1945, Paula was committed to Camarillo State Hospital. She was described as destitute in her committal hearing. Three doctors on the Psychopathic Commission said she was mentally ill and needed treatment. She was declared an opiate addict by one of the doctors that Carlyle had hired. Her own doctors denied the charge.

On Jan. 22, 1946, Paula lost yet another appeal for the $1000 a month alimony while she was still confined in Camarillo State Hospital.

On Aug. 2, 1946, the District Court of Appeal yet again denied Paula's plea for alimony and said the lower courts had not erred in refusing to award her alimony and that the refusal was due to the divorce which was granted to her husband on the grounds of "cruelty and infidelity." This appeal was based on the argument that she was sick during the first hearings and asked for them to be postponed but was denied, but the judge found no merit therein. The Times said Paula was still living in Camarillo State Hospital at this time, due to mental illness.

On April 17, 1958, Carlyle Thorpe had a heart attack at the age of 73, and died in Santa Barbara. He was one of the founders of Diamond Walnut Growers, Inc. and was called a millionaire in the headlines of his obituary. Carlyle was the general manager of the walnut growers organization in 1950, when he retired, and had managing it since its inception in 1912. During WWII, he was reportedly the chairman of the CA State Guayule Rubber Commission, which made rubber from the guayule plant. Carlyle's new wife, Maxine, was driving Carlyle to one of his ranches when he had the heart attack. His obituary also listed him as a "participant" in the "sensational suit" in which he divorced Paula. He was said to have left behind his widow Maxine, and 2 daughters and one son. Private funeral services were conducted in the "Wee Kirk o'the Heather" chapel at Forest Lawn Memorial Park, burial place of many wealthy and famous people in the Los Angeles area.
Author's Note: It seems somewhat tragic to me that it was easy to find Carlyle's obituary but no mention of whatever became of Paula is to be found. She seems to have died in anonymity inside Camarillo State Hospital,

as so many did. Their stories lead up to the hospital, then they evaporate. It is especially troubling since much of the testimony used against her to say she was an infidel was also countered by testimony from the people involved in the allegations, saying those claims were false. It is odd that Carlyle agreed that he had a prenuptial agreement for $425 a month for every month they stayed married, but I guess that is what his deal of $5000 he kept offering her in the divorce was about. I find it strange the courts did not demand he at least pay her the $425 a month for the years they were married, but perhaps the male judges felt the few thousand they awarded her in fees for her male attorneys took up that money. I wonder why she did not just dump this old man and do the same thing with some other old man her father's age who was looking for a young blonde on his arm. I wonder why she just did not get a new sugar daddy, so to speak. I wonder why it seems in her fight to get this one man's money, she seemed to actually drive herself mad and ended up in an insane asylum.

LATimes, Walnut Growers' Head Sued by Ex-Singer Wife, Jul. 21, 1943, p. 8.

LATimes, Carlyle Thorpe's Wife Collapses, Wins Alimony, Jul. 31, 1943, p. 3.

LATimes, Soldier Tells of Gay Party in Thorpe Case, Nov. 20, 1943, p. A12.

LATimes, Groom Testifies Thorpe's Wife Kissed Trainer, Nov. 24, 1943, p. 7.

LATimes, Thorpe Case Deposition Links Wife to Boy, 16, Nov. 27, 1943, p. A12.

LATimes, More Testimony Filed in Thorpe Divorce Case, Jan. 23, 1944, p. A8.

LATimes, Doctors Disagree on Illness of Mrs. Thorpe, So Judge Acts, Jan. 26, 1944, p. 10.

LATimes, Thorpes Were Married Twice, Wife Testifies, Mar. 24, 1944, p. A3.

LATimes, Thorpe Bedroom Scene Described by Daughter, Mar. 25, 1944, p. A3.

LATimes, Thorpe Asserts He Paid "Alimony" Since Wedding, Mar. 29, 1944, p. A16.

LATimes, Woman Detective Tells Thorpe Case Shadowing, Mar. 30, 1944, p. 5.

LATimes, Mother Denies Son Made Love to Mrs. Thorpe, Mar. 31, 1944, p. 12.

LATimes, Court Denies Alimony to Paula Thorpe, Aug. 12, 1944, p. A3.

LATimes, Paula Thorpe Near Death as Divorce Sequel, Feb. 16, 1945, p. 2.

LATimes, Los Angeles Briefs, Feb. 17, 1945, p. 5.

LATimes, Ex-Dancer Collapses at Alimony Hearing, Mar. 23, 1945, p. 3.

LATimes, Mrs. Thorpe Hysterical at Alimony Hearing, Mar. 23, 1945, p. A1.

LATimes, City Briefs, Mar. 24, 1945, p. 7.

LATimes, Paula Thorpe Plans New Try, Oct. 22, 1945, p. A3.

LATimes, Ex-Wife on Stretcher Seeks Thorpe Alimony, Oct. 23, 1945, p. 2.

LATimes, Paula Thorpe Sent to Hospital, Dec. 15, 1945, p. 4.

LATimes, Joan Crawford and Mate Part, Dec. 18, 1945, p. A1.

LATimes, Chamber Will Hold Annual Banquet Today, Jan. 23, 1946, p. A12.

LATimes, Paula Thorpe Loses Appeal, Aug. 3, 1946, p. A8.

LATimes, Rancher Carlyle Thorpe Dies of Heart Attack, Apr. 19, 1958, p. B1.

21 A YOUNG WOMAN WHO TOOK LSD AND THOUGHT SHE WAS A CHAIR

In July, 1966, the LATimes reported a woman was committed because she had taken LSD and was panicked because she "could not distinguish her body from the chair on which she was sitting." Later she said she "could not get back into" herself. After two days of Thorazine, which the Times referred to as "the most powerful tranquilizer known," she "calmed down." Talking about quintessential "bad trips," the Times reported seven people were committed to Camarillo or Metropolitan mental hospitals in April 1966 for LSD, and the General Hospital treated 23 others in April for LSD too. UCLA reported from Sept. 1965 – April 1966, they treated 70 people for acute reactions to LSD.

LATimes, George Reasons, Panic One of Gravest Perils Caused by LSD, Jul. 11, 1966, p. A1.

22 HAZEL YOUNGER

In 1967, Hazel's husband explains to the L.A. Times, "I signed some papers and they took her there after a short time of observation at County Hospital."

This is a very bizarre story where politicos ran Hazel Joyce Younger, a woman with a similar name to their political opponent, Mildred Younger, to admittedly confuse voters and win votes for their own candidate, incumbent CA Senator Tenney in 1954. The same man who entered Hazel's name in the running of the political race, Dr. Burgeson, also had Hazel committed to Camarillo State Mental Hospital for "menopausal psychosis" a year prior to him entering her name in the political race. When confronted with this paradox, Dr. Burgeson claimed he did not know she had been committed due to his letter asking she be committed and he claimed she seemed fine when he last visited her prior to filing for her to run for senate. This is the true tale of Hazel Younger, Camarillo State Mental Hospital, Dr. Samuel Burgeson and the 1954 CA Senate race.

Dr. Samuel D. Burgeson, of 761 S. Fetterley Ave, East Los Angeles, was a lead player in Senator Jack Tenney's campaign for reelection in the early 1950's. Burgeson was also the finance chairman for the Republican 19th Congressional District, and was nominated to the Republican County Central Committee. He was close friends with Senator Tenney and pictures of them playing music together at a piano, for example, were available to the public. Dr. Burgeson argued vehemently that he was anti-communist as was Senator Tenney, and said he ran Hazel Younger as an opponent to Mildred Younger, who was opposing Senator Tenney, because Mildred Younger was a communist and it was his duty as a Republican to confuse the vote between two women named Younger so that Tenney would be reelected.

Dr. Burgeson and Hazel's husband, Allen C. Younger, wrote a letter dated June 27, 1953, which recommended Hazel be committed to Camarillo State Hospital due to "menopausal psychosis." Allen Younger wrote in his letter about Hazel that she had been behaving strangely, that she was fearful and nervous, that she would get up at night and he would have to go find her, she was acting odd at work, and that she "talks constantly." Deputy Mental Hygiene Counselor Fred M. Cox signed a report saying Hazel had been knocked unconscious twice as a child, and later interviewed her while she was in restraints at the General Hospital. He reported she said she felt pain and fear most of the time. Two doctors, Dr. C. W. Olsen, and G. N. Thompson, also signed a certificate of examination stating Hazel was "a victim of involuntary psychosis and paranoid type schizophrenia associated with the change of life." Hazel Younger was examined in Psychopathic Court at the General Hospital on July 3, 1953 and due to reports by these men, Hazel Younger was sent to Camarillo Hospital as a mentally ill person, by Superior Court Judge William P. Houghton.

Hazel Younger was released from Camarillo State Hospital on Oct. 3, 1953 for an "extended home convalescence," and Dr. Burgeson prepared papers to run her in the senatorial race around the beginning of April, 1954. Dr. Burgenson said he had not spoken to Hazel Younger since he recommended she be committed on his doctor's prescription pad, and claimed he did not know she had been committed to Camarillo at his recommendation, and said when he did visit her in Spring of 1954 to discuss her run for office, she seemed "perfectly normal," which he defined as her being capable of doing household chores and raising children.

Dr. Burgeson filed the paperwork on behalf of Hazel Younger at the last hour. And after he filed her paperwork to run, she disappeared from her usual home at 431 S. Downey Road, East Los Angeles, and was said to have "fled" to avoid questions as to who she is and why she was all of a sudden running for political office with no political experience whatsoever. Investigations into this case showed that many of those who signed nominating petitions for Hazel to run later denied they signed the petitions that were filed with the Los Angeles County Registrar and said they had thought they were signing nominating petitions for Senator Tenney. Senator Tenney denied all knowledge of the matter. The L.A. Times had endorsed Senator Tenney several times before, but partially due to the outrage of this scandal, withdrew support for him, backing Mildred Younger instead.

On April 15, 1954, the Legislative Counsel Bureau asked for clarification in the case of Dr. Burgeson's running of Hazel Younger admittedly for deception. He testified repeatedly, and on numerous occasions, that the only reason Hazel Younger was running for the senate was to split the vote based on confusion over two women with the same name running against the incumbent. The Legislative Counsel Bureau said they felt Dr. Bergeson's actions amounted to fraud of the electoral process, and it was asked that Hazel Younger's name be taken off the ballot. By April 17, 1954, the Republican Executive Committee asked for an investigation into the filing of Hazel Younger on the ballot. The Westwood Young Republicans released a harsh statement of disapproval regarding the Tenney reelection tactics, and they also asked Hazel Younger to present herself for questioning as she was in hiding once the paperwork was filed. Many other Republican groups came forth to denounce these election tactics as well. A public condemnation of Dr. Burgeson was included in the Westwood Young Republicans statement and his tactics were condemned by many other local Republican groups as well.

On April 19, 1954, attorneys for Mildred Younger asked the CA Supreme Court to remove Hazel Younger's name from the senatorial ballot. It was argued Hazel was not a bona fide candidate and that she was "still under legal commitment to Camarillo State Hospital as insane." On April 20, 1954, Registrar of Voters, Benjamin S. Hite, cancelled Hazel Younger's voting privileges and asked the CA Supreme Court to remove her name from the senatorial ballot. Hite said Hazel's name was taken off the registered voters' list because she was committed to the state hospital as mentally ill and there was no record of her being "restored to capacity." (This conflicts with reports that say she was released in Oct. 1953, but corresponds with reports that she was still in the legal custody of Camarillo State Hospital, even though she was at home convalescing.)

In an L.A. Times article dated April 21, 1954, it was alleged that Hazel had been in hiding of her own volition or someone else's, that she was "concealed" since April 2, 1954, when her name was filed for the ballot, and that she never received a discharge from Camarillo Hospital. Affidavits filed with the state provided by names of petitioners for the nomination of Hazel Younger said they have never heard of Hazel Younger and were deceived into thinking they were signing petitions for Jack Tenney's reelection. On May 1, 1954, the CA Supreme Court by a 5 to 2 vote denied Mildred Younger's petition to have Hazel Younger's name taken off the June 8, 1954 primary ballot. The courts denied the removal of Hazel's name primarily because Hazel was missing, and could not be located to testify on her own behalf. The courts could not serve notice on Hazel for the hearing and most felt that

Hazel Younger needed to be present to state why she was running for senate, but she was not found by the time of this denial hearing. On June 3, 1954, the District Court of Appeals refused an appeal from Dr. Burgeson demanding he be placed on the Los Angeles County Republican Central Committee, due in part to his part in the Hazel Younger scandal.

On June 5, 1954, at 6 p.m., on nearly the eve of the election, Hazel Younger returned home from a 7 week "trip" in her dusty station wagon with her 3 young sons and husband. She refused to have her picture taken saying she had not been to a beauty parlor in 3 months. Her husband Allen, age 50, a shipping clerk, was driving while Hazel sat in the back seat and her husband answered questions. He said Hazel was tired and unsure of "just what she will do in the election." Her husband claimed she did not run to confuse voters but rather "she just took a notion to run," reports the L.A. Times. Allen did say that it was Dr. Burgeson that filed the electoral paperwork on Hazel's behalf and would not explain where their family had been since the filing of the paperwork in April. The L.A. Times reported it was obvious they had been camping and fishing and berry picking, due to camping gear in the car and boxes of berries and stained fingers of the children. But when asked, Allen said they "had just been away," according to the Times.

Allen Younger claimed the only reason his family had come home within days of the election with his wife's name was on the ballot, was because he had gotten word their mail delivery had stopped. He was unwilling to explain his family's hiding out for two months prior. Allen told the Times he was going to see Dr. Burgeson and after that meeting, they might have a public statement to offer the media. Allen claimed he had no idea what had happened since the family left their home right after the papers were filed for Hazel to run for office. Hazel's husband also made a statement vehemently arguing that his wife was not sent to Camarillo State Hospital for "craziness" but rather for "the change of life." Hazel's husband explains to the L.A. Times, "I signed some papers and they took her there after a short time of observation at County Hospital." Allen claimed his wife and he did not know Mildred Younger or Jack Tenney and that his wife merely wanted to "get into office and get something good done." As Allen spoke to the press from the driver's seat, Hazel sat in the back seat covering her face with a magazine while their 3 boys, Ellery, Arthur, and Keith, aged 4-8, played in the back seats as well. On the house door was still tacked the court subpoena for Hazel to appear in court in April 23, which may explain the family's quick disappearance for 2 months.

A day after Hazel returned to Los Angeles with her husband and 3 children from 2 months in hiding, she was reportedly back in hiding again. In an L.A.

Times article dated June 7, 1954, the headlines read, "Candidate Hazel Younger Goes Back into Hiding." This article refers to Hazel hiding behind religious tracts and her husband during the interview when they arrived home on the eve of June 5, and says her husband deferred all questions about his wife's candidacy, their strange disappearance for 2 months and the lack of any resemblance to a political campaign in Hazel's actions to Dr. Burgeson. It was reported that either Hazel or her husband had torn the court orders from their door upon their return and had thrown it on a porch chair, where it remained the day after the Youngers disappeared again. Dr. Burgeson had promised to release a statement about Hazel Younger's candidacy and his role in it, on June 6, 1954 at noon. Yet on June 6, he was "unavailable" and released no comment.

When the Youngers returned on the eve of June 5, they originally tried to deny they were the Younger family. The Times speculated that the Youngers may have thought the election had happened the week prior when they first returned, due to the timing of their return. Neither Hazel nor her husband would say where they had been when they were gone, but one of their sons said they had gone fishing in a place that sounded like Coronado and there was a Coronado pamphlet visible in the car. When asked who paid for their 2 month vacation, the husband evaded answering the question and he insisted he paid the filing fee for his wife's senatorial race, but did not know how much the fees were when asked. Senator Tenney also disavows all associations with Dr. Burgeson at this point in the press, as well.

On June 8, 1954, Hazel and Allen Younger entered their polling place to vote. They appeared at 6:35 p.m. with the polls closing at 7 p.m. Allen Younger was allowed to vote, Hazel was not. Due to the April 21 revocation of her voting rights by the Registrar of Voters, Benjamin Hite. Dr. Burgeson was still not available for comments he had promised on his role in the Hazel Younger case after he voted on June 8. In the end, Mildred Younger did run as the GOP candidate for senator in 1954, but lost to Richard Richards, a Democrat. It would not be until 1976 that the first female Senate member was elected. Dr. Burgeson died in 1959 at age 58 from a car accident. His 1959 obituary reads that his terms as Republican state committeeman would have ended a few months after his death, and said that he retired from his post as a Los Angeles Police and Fire Department surgeon after 15 years at that job in 1955, just after the Hazel Younger scandal, though no mention of the scandal appears in his obituary. At his death, he was said to leave a widow, 2 daughters, 2 sisters and 4 grandchildren.

I do not know what happened to Hazel after June 1954, and there are not any obituaries I can find for her in the press and the story of her seems to end with the senator scandal. I find it ironic that Dr. Burgeson stayed in politics after the Hazel Younger scandal, but that he died by accident almost 5 years exactly from the date that he filed the paperwork to nominate Hazel for office. We can find more information about Burgeson, and his death, but none of his negative plots and ploys were discussed or memorialized. We can also find information about Mildred Younger with an easy Google search. But when you Google Hazel Younger, there is no entry for this story of her life of commitment to Camarillo State by her husband and Dr. Burgeson for "menopausal psychosis." There is no ending to this story in terms of Hazel either. She was a pawn in big boys' games and her record is silent. So, here's to you, Hazel Younger, and to getting your name in its rightful place in Google search engines and historical archives.

LATimes, Hazel Younger Returns, Won't Discuss Politics, Jun. 6, 1954, p. 1.

LATimes, Former Mental Patient in Race to Aid Tenney, Apr. 9, 1954, p. 1.

LATimes, Political Trickery Seen in Second Mrs. Younger Filing, Apr. 8, 1954, p. 4.

LATimes, Tenney Backers' Chicanery Exposed, Apr. 10, 1954, p. A4.

LATimes, Order to Put Hazel Younger Off Ballot Seen, Apr. 16, 1954, p. 5.

LATimes, Hazel J. Younger Filing Probe Asked, Apr. 17, 1954, p. A1.

LATimes, State Supreme Court Asked to Bar Hazel Younger from Primary Ballot, Apr. 20, 1954, p. 4.

LATimes, Hazel Younger Taken Off Registered Voters' List, Apr. 21, 1954, p. A1.

LATimes, Court Keeps Hazel Younger on June Ballot, May 1, 1954, p. 1.

LATimes, GOP Seating Plea Lost by Burgeson, Jun. 3, 1954, p. 22.

LATimes, Hazel Younger Returns, Won't Discuss Politics, Jun. 6, 1954, p. 1.

LATimes, Hazel Younger Returns, Won't Discuss Politics, Jun. 6, 1954, p. 1.

LATimes, Hazel Younger Returns, Won't Discuss Politics, Jun. 6, 1954, p. 1.

LATimes, Hazel Younger Returns, Won't Discuss Politics, Jun. 6, 1954, p. 1.

LATimes, Candidate Hazel Younger Goes Back into Hiding, Jun. 7, 1954, p. 1.

LATimes, Candidate Hazel Younger Goes Back into Hiding, Jun. 7, 1954, p. 1.

LATimes, Hazel Younger Appears; Not Allowed to Vote, Jun. 9, 1954, p. 7.

LATimes Obituaries, Mildred Younger, 86, GOP Activist, Wife of Former State Attorney, Dies, Nov. 16, 2006 (http://articles.latimes.com/2006/nov/16/local/me-younger16/2, as retrieved on Dec. 26, 2010).

LATimes, Dr. Burgeson Rites Set, Feb. 26, 1959, p. B6.

23 MRS. VIRGINIA EVELYN WILSON

In 1967, Mrs. Virginia Evelyn Wilson, aged 61, was convicted of murdering her son, Joel D. Wilson, aged 21. Her son was an airman in the military who was bound for Vietnam. His mother killed him because she said she "feared he might be captured and tortured by the Viet Cong." Virginia was declared insane by the courts and spent almost 2 years at Camarillo State Hospital. On Dec. 10, 1968, Virginia was set free after a Santa Monica Court hearing because she was "certified mentally competent."

Los Angeles Times, "Mother Freed in Son's Shooting," Dec. 11, 1968, p. B8.

ABOUT THE AUTHOR

Kirsten Anderberg earned her Master's Degree in CA History and Archiving at CA State University at Northridge in 2011, and has her Bachelor's Degree in Political Science from the University of WA in Seattle. She has published the first book ever on the topic of MacLaren Hall, a child protection institution in Los Angeles which was open from the 1940's until 2003. She was also a resident of MacLaren Hall as an 8 year old child in 1969. Her research on institutional history and society's "unwanted" led her to Camarillo State Mental Hospital, near her home in Ventura, CA. MacLaren Hall and Camarillo shared many of the same doctors and "treatments." Kirsten has written about activism which came out of the East Coast U.S., which is putting names on numbered graves behind mental hospitals. She is an historical speaker on the topic of institutional history and received a fellowship from the Historical Society of Southern CA in 2009 for her MacLaren Hall research and writings.

You can contact the author at kirstena@resist.ca.

For more of Kirsten's writing, visit www.kirstenanderberg.com.

Made in the USA
San Bernardino, CA
30 August 2018